WIRED

for Ministry

WIRED

for Ministry

How the Internet,
Visual Media, and Other
New Technologies Can
Serve Your Church

JOHN P. JEWELL

Brazos Press
A Division of Baker Book House Co
Grand Rapids, Michigan 49516

Published by Brazos Press
a division of Baker Book House Company
P.O. Box 6287, Grand Rapids, MI 49516-6287
www.brazospress.com

Printed in the United States of America

Library of Congress Cataloging-in-Publication Data

Jewell, John P., 1938-
    Wired for ministry : how the Internet, visual media, and other new technologies can serve your church / John P. Jewell.
        p.   cm.
    Includes bibliographical references.
    ISBN 1-58743-075-4 (pbk.)
    1. Internet—Religious aspects—Christianity. 2. Church work—Audio-visual aids. 3. Church work—Data processing. I. Title.
BV652.77.J495 2004
254′.3—dc21
                                        2003012191

For

Martha Jo Schelling

and

John P. Jewell Sr.

'til we meet again

Contents

Part 3 Study the Practice

Foreword

In his previous book, *New Tools For A New Century: First Steps In Equipping Your Church For The Digital Revolution*, John Jewell gave congregations an indispensable introduction to the technological resources now available to expand and support ministry. I have heartily recommended it to resistant church secretaries, harried pastors, and frustrated worship leaders who are not only intimidated by the accelerating rate of technological change, but also bewildered as to how to fulfill the demands that the church embody these advances. Dr. Jewell's book, with its disarming humor, which never condescends, patiently guides people through the basics of computers, software, and Internet use. In addition, he is able to explain developments in technology in a way that is convincing both to those who remember when television began and those who cannot remember typewriters!

One theme of that earlier book was of special importance: theological reflection on technology as either servant or master in the church. Peppered throughout the tutorials on PowerPoint, the hints for introducing media arts in worship, and the directions to tantalizing websites were constant reminders of the dangers of imposing technology on people and programs. In his new book, Dr. Jewell explores this theme more thoroughly. He helpfully distinguishes between the Internet as a *factor in contemporary communication* of the gospel and the mistaken view that it is a *foundation of the church's proclamation*.

Attention to theological seriousness in the relationship between ministry and technology makes this book a rare find in the midst of Protestant pragmatism. John Jewell can actually speak and write "technobabble" but refuses to do so. Instead, he takes readers by the hand, whether they are tyros or "techies," and shows them that technology raises basic questions about how people are connected in the community of the body of Christ.

Given the explosion of information available on the Internet, theological discernment is necessary as never before. If religious bookstores (in addition to their benefits) flooded the market with questionable religious products, then the arrival of the Internet multiplies that problem tenfold. Church members can easily access numerous religious websites (many of them of dubious origin) and bring printed copies to their local Bible study. This presents both challenge and opportunity for clergy and lay leaders of congregations to help their members begin to question the sources of websites and their theological assumptions about the role of technology in the acquisition of knowledge—not necessarily identical with information—about their faith.

I recommend this book to any pastor who has had to respond to parishioners who, on the one hand, insist that "we must get all the church officers on e-mail now," and those, on the other hand, who warn that Bill Gates is the Antichrist and they know this because they read it in an e-mail! John Jewell gives us sound strategies for bringing sanity to ministry settings overcome by the serious and silly claims that assail us in the Information Age.

However, this book is more than a theological study of the challenges to ministry that come with the emerging digital technology. You will learn here how basic educational and organizational ministries of your church can be enhanced. You will find tools to launch evangelistic outreach and church planting. You will catch a glimpse of how churches can extend their ministries beyond their doors to the Internet itself. You will discover how the role of technology in worship may either "enable or disable" the congregation's perception of the message being proclaimed. Most importantly, over and over again, this book brings us to the place where guidelines and processes for engaging technology are integrated with basic principles of Christian ministry. As Dr. Jewell puts it (and notice the strategic order of his claim): "*Who* we are in Christ shapes *how* we are in the world." Or, as one of his students put it: we need to learn "how to do technology so it doesn't do us."

Finally, a word about John Jewell's credibility and authority to be our teacher. With over thirty years in the pastorate, he can speak with intimate knowledge of the day-to-day struggles of the local church. As one of his colleagues at the University of Dubuque Theological Seminary, I have been the recipient of his teaching and preaching and sincerely wish I had had his guidance when I was pastoring churches. John also brings to this book his expertise as a programmer and systems analyst. (Don't miss his wise spiritual advice in chapter 13 on how he, as a technology professional who wants to be a "totally connected Christian leader," practices "technology fasting.") Of special significance for his readers will be the case studies he shares from the congregations and students he has worked with in his role as director of instructional technology and distance learning here at the seminary. All in all, John is a gifted pastor-teacher who has been placed by God's providence in the midst of the digital revolution as salt and light for the rest of us.

Leicester R. Longden
Associate Professor of Evangelism and Discipleship
University of Dubuque Theological Seminary

Acknowledgments

I am grateful for my friends and colleagues at the University of Dubuque Theological Seminary who have provided the lively and nourishing community where this book took shape. A deep love for the local church and a commitment to preparing competent, faithful pastors has helped to sharpen the concerns and issues that form the heart of this work.

This book could not have been written without the support and encouragement of Bradley Longfield, our seminary dean, and Ann Hoch, associate dean. Elmer Colyer offered helpful insights at the very beginning of this project. Les Longden and Phil Jamieson have both contributed to the text.

Corrie Aukema, my work-study student, brought her keen copyediting skills, offered helpful suggestions, and helped to move this project along much more promptly than would have been the case without her assistance. Nicky Story, my program assistant, and Julie Mulcahey, my secretary, have frequently gone beyond the call of duty in keeping our department on top of things in a rapidly changing environment. Nicky has been my resident "Gen N" sounding board.

Rodney Clapp has given helpful insight and encouragement during the process of bringing this manuscript to maturity.

For all these friends and coworkers, I am grateful to God.

Finally, for my wife Janell and daughter Jennifer, I am constantly giving thanks to God. Their support and understanding during long evenings when I could not spare much more than a hug and brief evening prayers have blessed me with much grace.

Soli Deo Gloria.

John Jewell
February 17, 2003

Introduction

> We've all heard that a million monkeys banging on a mil-
> lion typewriters will eventually reproduce the entire works
> of Shakespeare. Now, thanks to the Internet, we know this
> is not true.[1]
>
> Robert Wilensky, University of California

No one can seriously challenge the fact that digital technology and its favorite child, the Internet, have profoundly changed our world. Whether or not we are personally involved in the use of computers, e-mail, or PDAs (personal digital assistants), none of us has escaped the impact of technology. The digital revolution has muscled its way into our economic, social, physical, intellectual, and even spiritual lives. Even if I did not own a personal computer, my 401k could still have a stake in technology stocks. If I were a technology holdout who still did not have an e-mail account, my surgeon might very well receive medical records from my internist via an e-mail attachment or fax machine. Even those who do not care for all this "computer stuff" could still find themselves viewing a PowerPoint presentation with notes and pictures of the Holy Land during the pastor's sermon on Sunday.

There was a time during the late 2000 and early 2001 dot-com bust when people wondered whether the technological revolution had come to an end. Thousands of dot-coms failed, and almost none of us who had a pension plan escaped the blow to our retirement funds. There was a bit of "I told you so" on the part of technology naysayers, but talk of the end of the digital revolution was premature. The revolution did not stop, it simply began to mature. The time had come for what many people call "B2R," or "Back to Reality." Nevertheless, Yahoo and Amazon are still around in spite of an enormous shakeout of failed companies; Amazon has had its first profitable quarter since its inception, and a new website joins the Internet every four seconds.[2]

The church, especially in the mainline, has lagged behind in getting on board with opportunities that are available for mission and ministry through the use of new technologies. But this is changing. A growing number of voices call for reaching the world for Christ, engaging the younger generation, and bringing new life to worship, all through the power of new technologies. These voices urge the church to heed the call of God and use the tools of the digital revolution to fulfill the Great Commission.[3] Increasingly sophisticated technologies for Web-based ministry and media arts in ministry are being used by some churches with a significant impact on their communities.[4]

In spite of all these good things, it is critically important to raise a strong caution about the dangers of buying into an inflated view of technology. The technological revolution of the past two decades, which has gone into all-out sprint mode in the past five years, is an amazing event in human history. It has brought about a whole new suite of tools that have great potential to enhance the ministries of the church. However, technology is a means, not an answer for everything that ails the church. It brings new possibilities, but not new basic principles to the life of the church. Technology provides new tools, but not new theology.

Consider this assessment of the impact of the Internet for the church:

> There are watershed events that shape human history: the Fall, the Flood, the crucifixion and resurrection of Jesus Christ, and Pentecost. After those events, nothing was the same. . . . Today we live during one of those life-altering historic events that is being orchestrated by God. This is the Internet moment in human history. From now on, nothing will be the same. . . . What we do with the Internet is as important as what we do in the pulpit.[5]

Personally, I am not quite ready to equate the advent of the Internet to the resurrection of Jesus Christ or with Pentecost. The pulpit, insofar as it reflects the apostolic proclamation of the historic church, is a foundation of the church. The Internet has indeed brought about amazing changes in our world, and what we do with the Internet is important. The Internet is a *factor* in contemporary communication of the Good News of Jesus Christ, but it is not a *foundation* of the church's proclamation. The pervasiveness of the Internet does not even come close to the power of a faithful pulpit.

Another author suggests that the very nature of church has changed:

> In scores of Internet chat rooms, people and computers now "go to church" together. It is not the kind of church to which most of us are accustomed. Nevertheless, people—and perhaps computers?—*are* experiencing worship within these Internet churches. And young people, especially teenagers, are often leading these online congregations—with the assistance of their computer software programs, of course.[6]

The Internet has potential for bringing a sense of community to people who may be distant from a physical worshiping community; it may even extend the possibilities of community for a local church. But people *and* computers experiencing worship in a chat room? I am relatively comfortable stating that this is most likely not what the Psalmist had in mind when the words were first spoken, "I was glad when they said unto me; let us go into the house of the LORD" (Ps. 122:1 KJV).

All of this begs the question of how the church can make the most efficient use of this new gift of technology. Three basic themes in the field of ministry and technology are important in the attempt to answer this question. The first is to have a clear understanding of the difference between tools, which *enable* connection between people, and the actual *connecting*, which leads to community. I discuss this as the issue of "Connectivity and Connection." The second theme is the difference between the issue of technological methods by which the Good News is delivered and genuine communication in which the Good News is heard and embraced. I will address this as the issue of "Transportation and Communication." The third theme has to do with "Chaos and Community." Without proper understanding of the relationship between ministry and technology, digital capabilities and discipleship, technology tends to get imposed *on* ministry rather than integrated *into* ministry. Instead of nourishing and building up the community, it screeches across the church like fingernails across a chalkboard.

Connectivity and Connection

Early in the afternoon of December 7, 1941, Secretary of War Henry Stimson called President Franklin D. Roosevelt and informed him that the Empire of Japan had attacked Pearl Harbor. The next day President Roosevelt delivered his famous "Day of Infamy" speech to a joint session of Congress and a national radio audience. Never had the nation been more connected than it was the day hundreds of thousands listened to their president's six-minute speech in which he declared, "No matter how long it may take us to overcome this premeditated invasion, the American people will in their righteous might win through to absolute victory."[7]

Roosevelt connected with the nation using a relatively young technology. NBC had arrived on the scene only fifteen years earlier with forty-eight affiliate stations. CBS with its initial forty-seven affiliates was only thirteen years old. Radio was America's primary medium of connectivity in 1935. Two-thirds of the country's homes had a radio in 1935, and yet it was not until 1940 that radio news reached maturity, only a year before the "Day of Infamy" speech.[8] In his speech, Roosevelt told Congress and the American people that war would be declared so that, "this form of treachery shall never endanger us again."[9]

About sixty years later, a treachery beyond anything Roosevelt or 1941 America could ever imagine rocked the nation as the Twin Towers of the World Trade Center in New York came crashing to the ground along with the worldview of millions of Americans. New technologies connected the country and indeed the whole world. Within moments, pictures of shock and disbelief on the faces of people around the world flashed across television sets and scrolled across our computer screens.

I was working at my desk on the computer when a news alert popped up on my screen, "WORLD TRADE CENTER ATTACKED!" I clicked on the headline for "the full story," and read with almost total disbelief what was unfolding before the eyes of the world in real time.

There is a critically important clue to the use of technology in ministry that is just beneath the surface of these two episodes in American history.

Franklin D. Roosevelt's six-minute radio address helped to connect a nation in just under twenty-four hours. On September 11, 2001, America and the world were connected within moments. Something tells us, however, that the "connection" people felt in America when President Roosevelt addressed the nation was different from the "connection" that took place within minutes of the Twin Towers being attacked.

We get to this difference by examining two distinct ways the word "connect" is used in this discussion. When I use my computer to go to the Internet, I click on my "Internet connection" logo and am soon "connected." (If I have cable access I am always "connected.") There is another meaning to the word "connected." Perhaps you and I discover in an initial conversation that we share common interests, values, and goals. You could say we made a "connection." Connection means two different things in these examples, and the difference is of paramount importance when we talk about the use of technological tools for the enhancement of ministry.

It is helpful to make a distinction between the issue of technological connection and personal connection. Radio, television, computers, wires, and cables are actually tools that provide "connectivity." These tools can enable connection, but they cannot provide connection. Connectivity has to do with technological tools and resources. The progression from Johannes Gutenberg's printing press to telegraph, radio, television, and the Internet has provided increasingly swift connectivity. A graph showing the speed of connectivity from Gutenberg's time to our own would show a remarkable rise from years, to weeks, to days, to hours, to nanoseconds (a billionth of a second).[10]

Connection, on the other hand, has to do with relationships and community. Connection, or relationship and community building, is a fundamental task of Christian ministry. The use of computers and technology in the church provides us with additional opportunities for building connections. But the technology does not guarantee connection and may even create barriers to building authentic community. There is much work to do with the difference between "connectivity" and "connection" for those of us who labor in the field of technology and ministry.

According to my grandmother and others from her generation, authentic connection took place when President Roosevelt addressed the nation. America was a nation hungry for leadership in the face of crisis. The radio provided connectivity; Roosevelt's leadership provided connection. On September 11, 2001, television, and more notably, the Internet, provided connectivity. Information flooded the country and the world—overwhelming information. But was it authentic connection? There was some connection, some confusion, and lots of chaos. Mainly, we were overwhelmed.

Connectivity in 1941 America was much slower than it is today, but connection between Americans took place in a relatively short period of time. Conversely, connectivity in 2001 America was light years ahead in speed, but it is not certain whether or not authentic community ever really resulted from the flood of information. In 1941, America was involved and committed. In 2001, America was informed and concerned. The difference between connectivity and connection is critically instructive for our discussion of ministry and technology in a connected world. Indeed, we are closer to the truth in calling it a "(dis)connected" world.

Transportation and Communication

Do you remember the Pony Express? No doubt you have seen those old western movies where Pony Express riders endured more than any contemporary mail delivery person can imagine. Try this quick quiz. How long was the Pony Express in operation? Do you think maybe twenty or thirty years? The image is such an important part of our perception of America's western expansion that many think that the Pony Express was around for some time. It wasn't.

The Pony Express was in existence for a mere nineteen months. It came and went more quickly than a dot-com bust. The Pony Express was in service from April 1860 to November 1861. Its primary mission was to deliver mail and news between St. Joseph, Missouri, and San Francisco, California. Riders were hired, horses purchased, and large investments made. The speed of the Pony Express was amazing for its time. The following news story was printed in *The Weekly West*, published in St. Joseph, Missouri, on April 7, 1860, in an article called, "The Greatest Enterprise of Modern Times!!"

The rider is a Mr. Richardson, formerly a sailor, and a man accustomed to every description of hardship, having sailed for years amid the snows and icebergs of the Northern ocean. He was to ride last night the first stage of forty miles, changing horses once, in five hours; and before this paragraph meets the eyes of our readers, the various dispatches contained in the saddlebags, which left here at dark last evening, will have reached the town of Marysville, on the Big Blue, one hundred and twelve miles distant — an enterprise never before accomplished even in this proverbially fast portion of the country.[11]

Yet, despite significant press coverage, the Pony Express never turned a profit. It began with a flurry of media hype and ended up losing $200,000 (almost four million dollars in 2002 money). What happened? On June 16, 1860, about ten weeks after the Pony Express began operations, Congress authorized a bill instructing the secretary of the treasury to subsidize the building of a transcontinental telegraph line to connect the Missouri River and the Pacific Coast. On October 26, 1861, the telegraph line reached the west coast, and San Francisco was in direct contact with New York City. On that day the Pony Express was officially terminated.[12]

The central lesson to be learned from the Pony Express is that it is absolutely essential to stay centered in your primary purpose. The Pony Express was a child of the transportation industry. Its founders were the leaders of the Stage Coach era. When the Pony Express entered the communication business, it completely missed the obvious point that the overland telegraph system would make communication via Pony Express obsolete.

There is a parallel for those of us who work in the area of technology and ministry. Technology is in the "transportation" business. It processes and delivers information. Ministry has more to do with "communication." Slick transport without substantive communication will no more advance the Good News than the romantic appeal of the Pony Express could outrun the telegraph. In other words, it is important to stay on target with the task of communicating the content of the faith even while we use increasingly impressive technological tools to deliver that content.

Chaos and Community

The biblical drama begins as God brings order out of chaos and creation out of a formless void. Before order and creation, however, the Spirit of God was "moving" over the surface of deep waters. The New Revised Standard Version reads, "a wind from God swept over the face of the waters." The root word for moving or hovering is "brooding." The New International Version Bible Commentary has this interesting slant on Genesis 1:2: "The second part of v. 2 describes the work of God, or the Spirit of God, in the initial stages of Creation, hovering over the world like an eagle 'hovering' over its young with great concern."[13]

I have been an enthusiastic and early adopter of the use of computer-age technological tools in my ministry for a little over two decades. Actually, use of technology in ministry is not a new thing at all. Anyone who has ever shown a film strip or presented a slide show in church has used technology. But . . . something new is going on with digital technologies and computer- enhanced ministry. Something that should have us "brooding" over the whole field of ministry and technology, "like an eagle hovering over its young with great concern."

The University of Dubuque Theological Seminary began a program for a Certificate in Ministry and Technology in the summer of 2001. A group of ten pastors formed the inaugural class, which included two on-campus residencies; a year of online learning, research, and projects; as well as a final project that will make a significant contribution to the life of the church in the area of ministry and technology. One of the assignments for the group during an online Web ministry learning module was to visit the websites of several churches. A member of the group summarized it well when he said, "After an hour I could not handle it any more. I saw more ugly and bad than good. Most did not inspire me to want to know more about the church or return to the site." An online discussion ensued as to whether there should be some kind of regulation against ugly church websites.

A conversation with a college student is another example of the great concerns I have with the field of ministry and technology. She was telling me how much she liked her new pastor.

> "He's really cool," she exclaimed.
> "That's great," I answered. "What is it you like about him?"

"He's really into computers and stuff. Last Sunday he did a bunch of PowerPoint slides and used a film clip in the sermon. It was excellent!"

It was evident that her pastor's use of technology had impressed her.

"Sound's interesting." I replied. "What was the sermon about?"

"I don't know," she answered, "but it was way better than the boring sermons our last pastor used to give."

She went on to say that some of the older folks in the congregation were blown away by the whole thing, but the kids liked it. Her focus was on the tools instead of the message. There was connectivity but no real connection. Older people in the congregation did not connect because the technology was a barrier, and the young woman did not connect because she focused on technology while completely forgetting the message. "Ugly" and uninviting websites as well as "cool" and forgotten sermons lead to this conclusion. The issue for ministry is not whether technology should be used but how it should be used.

When the use of technological tools does not bring about authentic connection in the congregation, the end result is not neutral, it is chaos. The amazing potential of technological tools to enhance community is matched by the amazing potential of these same tools to engender chaos.

In the church, the only real measure of the success of technology is its ability to enhance the quality of community. Community, or the quality of the life of the body of Christ, is a critical and biblically mandated foundation for ministry. If there is no unified, connected community, there is no viable body of Christ to reach the world. Community unites and chaos divides. Division in the body of Christ is a central concern of Paul in his first letter to the Corinthian Church.

Indeed, the body does not consist of one member but of many. If the foot would say, "Because I am not a hand, I do not belong to the body," that would not make it any less a part of the body. And if the ear would say, "Because I am not an eye, I do not belong to the body," that would not make it any less a part of the body. If the whole body were an eye, where would the hearing be? If the whole body were hearing, where would the sense of smell be? But as it is, God arranged the members in the body, each one of them, as he chose. . . . (1 Cor. 12:14–18)

The ability to use technological tools in the life of the community can be a gift from God that assists in the healthy functioning of the body. Or, it may be an occasion for division in the body. It can bring about chaos or it can help build community. Later in 1 Corinthians, Paul points to the one thing that can keep things on track. "I will show you a still more excellent way. If I speak in the tongues of mortals and of angels, but do not have love, I am a noisy gong or a clanging cymbal" (1 Cor. 12:31–13:1).

For the purposes of this book, I would reword this something like, "Though I enhance my sermons with PowerPoint and e-mail the entire church membership on a daily basis, but do not enhance the quality of community, I am a digital flash or an electronic annoyance."

A Chastened Embracement of Technology for Ministry

In spite of all the difficulties inherent in using technology in ministry, I remain evangelical in my pursuit of ways to enhance ministry, build community, and strengthen the church with the aid of technology. This is territory into which we must continue to venture. The spies have gone in to examine the technology landscape, and it is a good land. There are indeed giants in the land and these giants represent obstacles to be overcome, but it is still a good land. There are wonderful ways that technology can help us do things we could not do or do as effectively in the past. With the help of God and the abiding presence of the Spirit of God, we can make use of the powerful potential of new technologies in the cause of ministry. I invite you to explore with me some of the pitfalls and promises of this field.

I have spent the last three-and-a-half years working full time in the young field of ministry and technology after spending thirty years in parish ministry. It is humbling to realize that I have made most of the mistakes that form the reflective and sometimes cautious core of this book. It is my hope that this work will advance the church's dialogue about the way current and emerging technologies can engage the promise of technology while avoiding the pitfalls. The Internet, along with all the new technologies that have been spawned by faster and smaller microchips, are a part of every Christian's daily life. This holds great promise for the integration of ministry and technology in a way that can bring about authentic connection in a disconnected world.

This book addresses three overarching themes that will help the reader discern appropriate ways to integrate new technologies in ministry. These three themes form the three parts of the book.

1. We need to be aware of the pitfalls of the new technologies in the life of the Christian community.
2. We need to develop a knowledge of the promise of new technologies that can facilitate and enrich ministry.
3. We need to develop a working strategy for the implementation of the best practices for the integration of technology in ministry.

My prayerful hope is that this book will assist pastors, youth leaders, and involved, committed Christians in churches across the country to make discerning use of the rich new resources God has made possible through technology. The book is not just for those Christian leaders and congregations that will make technology a central focus in ministry. It is for every church or ministry and its leaders, because technology can make a significant contribution in almost every ministry context.

Part 1

Be Aware of the Pitfalls

| 1 |

The Regressive Potential
of Technology
in the Church

. . . technological satisfaction contributes to the sense that we are living in a world that is increasingly superficial, disposable, and that routinely turns luxuries into necessities, and that catapults us from one faddish imperative to the next without time for introspection.[1]

Susan J. White

At the beginning of all things the Word of God calls the heavens and the earth into being. The Word creates life, gives guidance to the people of God through the law and the prophets, and calls the people of God to repentance and renewal when they have turned away from the Word. Finally, the drama of redemption is fulfilled when, "the Word became flesh and lived among us, and we have seen his glory, the glory as of a father's only son, full of grace and truth" (John 1:14).

29

The essential power of God's Word living among us in the flesh is that *this* Word is incarnational and relational. The previous law was good, Paul says; it was our "tutor to lead us to Christ, that we may be justified by faith. But now that faith has come, we are no longer under a tutor" (Gal. 3:24–25 NASB).

The Christian's faith relationship with God in Christ is made complete in fellowship where the incarnational Word is at the heart of the community. The First Letter of John expresses the intimacy of life in fellowship with the incarnate Word:

> We declare to you what was from the beginning, what we have heard, what we have seen with our eyes, what we have looked at and touched with our hands, concerning the word of life—this life was revealed, and we have seen it and testify to it, and declare to you the eternal life that was with the Father and was revealed to us—we declare to you what we have seen and heard so that you also may have fellowship with us; and truly our fellowship is with the Father and with his Son Jesus Christ. (1 John 1:1–3)

In the biblical drama, the Word, which binds the people of God to their Creator, moves from law, to prophetic word, to flesh. The Word made flesh gathers a community energized by the Spirit of God where Christ is present in a fellowship of persons. One of the key themes of this book is that, insofar as technology enables and enhances this incarnational and relational character of Christian fellowship, it has the potential for great good. However, when technology is improperly understood and inappropriately applied, it becomes regressive and moves the community of faith away from its relational nature. Put another way, preaching is at its best when the preacher becomes transparent to the Word of God, and the fellowship is engaged by the Holy Spirit and nourished toward maturity in Christ. So also, when technological resources are properly applied, the technology becomes transparent to the living Word and the church is nourished.

There are two characteristics that alert us to regressive potential in the use of technological tools. When either or both of these characteristics are operative in the church it is very likely that the result will be regressive. These marks of regression are: (1) when technology is intrusive and (2) when technology is messianic.

When Technology Is Intrusive

A prime example of intrusive technology is the cell phone. Most of us have heard cell phones go off in restaurants, theaters, meetings, and even worship. A United Methodist pastor wrote about his experience with cell phone interruption in a letter to the *St. Petersburg Times Tech News*.

> One Sunday, we were hardly past the consecration and were distributing the bread at Communion when behind me the cell phone of my liturgist/ reader went off. Now, she doesn't just have a ringer. She has a tune, the William Tell Overture, as her enunciator. It went off like a cannon shot in the hallowed silence of the sanctuary, while folks were receiving the Body of Christ. She tried to silence it by scrunching it up to her chest, but she couldn't stifle it enough to keep everyone from hearing the whole theme as she slunk out of the chancel into the sacristy to take the call. Though she muttered under her breath, we all could hear her still.[2]

Cell phones are products of superb technology and are not inherently intrusive. Yet most of us have been irritated by cell phones in restaurants, movie theaters, and automobiles. A cell phone left on during worship wins the owner the inconsiderate prize. This device can turn sacred space into just another place where the aggravation of a hectic world intrudes.

It is true that unlike an LCD (liquid crystal display) projector, cell phones are not intended to be carried into worship in order to enhance worship. Perhaps they should be checked at the door, but other applications of technology that *are* intended to enhance worship have frequently proven as intrusive as the William Tell Overture.[3]

One example of an older, predigital technology illustrates how something helpful can also be a hindrance. Many of us worship in sanctuaries that are equipped with a sound system. When these systems are working properly, they are an absolutely wonderful aid to worship. However, almost everyone has been in worship one time or another when the sound system was sitting on the edge of a loud squeal. The tip-off was a faint high-pitched hum while someone was speaking or singing. You found yourself on edge, hoping someone was on their way to turn down the volume before the congregation was treated to an ear-shattering screech. Sound systems can create noises that rank right up there with the protestations of an angry Siamese cat!

But what about those wonderful computer-mediated presentations that bring new possibilities to worship? There are film clips, PowerPoint sermon outlines, and hymns projected on giant screens. This is all good, isn't it?

The short answer is, "Yes, it is good—or at least *mostly* good." But, there is an important issue to raise here that will be discussed in more detail later in the book. There are churches that can specialize in using sophisticated technologies in the production of amazing worship experiences. These services speak to a large number of people who are blessed by their experience. The budget in these larger congregations frequently includes line items for full-time technology staff. The financial commitment to technological resources for ministry is a major factor in the success of their efforts. The reality is, most congregations and judicatories do not have the kind of economic muscle that is required to develop sophisticated technology-driven ministries. Yet there is much that can be done to enhance educational worship and other ministry areas with modest budget requirements. This book is written for the mainstream church that does not have large budget support for the integration of technology and ministry—much less sufficient funds to hire full-time technology staff. In fact, when you reach the end of this book you may discover that smaller congregations sometimes just might be able to do it better.

It is especially important to ensure that technology is not intrusive when working with a small budget and less expensive equipment. It can be done well and with good results, but beware of an outcome like the one that happened to one of my students. She planned to use a film clip and PowerPoint slides as a part of a Lenten series in the small congregation where she was the student pastor. She was able to borrow an LCD projector from the local library and produced a wonderful PowerPoint presentation on the creation account in the first chapter of Genesis on her laptop computer. I previewed the presentation for her, and the work was excellent. It could have been a part of a meaningful experience.

The excited pastor told her mostly older congregation that this would be a special Lenten service, but didn't say just *how* it would be special. On the day of the service, the pastor arrived early to set up the sanctuary.

However, she did not allow quite enough time to find a working outlet, secure a long enough extension cord, hook up the laptop computer and VCR to the projector, adjust the length from the projector to the screen (based on the "throw" of the LCD projector's lens), check for sound, and preview the entire presentation. Also, although the LCD on loan from the library was a good projector, it did not exactly match the projector the pastor learned to use at the seminary. When the congregation began to enter the sanctuary, the pastor was still hooking up components, but she was able to start only five minutes late. Next, when it came time for the presentation, the computer had frozen up, and she had to reboot the system. Finally, the first PowerPoint slide appeared, but it was out of focus and the music that was supposed to accompany the slides wasn't there. After another five minute delay, the presentation started and everything was great—for eight minutes. When it came time for the VCR clip, it turned out that the tape was not located in exactly the right place, and in the stress of the moment, the pastor forgot whether her clip was before or after the scene that appeared on the screen. Giving up on the media-assisted message, the pastor gave her message verbally and described for the congregation how the service had been designed and what it was meant to convey.

What was the inevitable result? "We don't need none of that newfangled computer stuff around here . . ." one of the deacons suggested.

Instead of the positive impact she expected, three main drawbacks took the congregation's attention away from this pastor's message and focused it onto the means by which she tried to convey it.

- She failed to prepare her audience, resulting in surprise, and for some, dismay.
- She did not allow sufficient time for on-site preparation, which led to a time delay.
- She did not establish adequate familiarity with the materials and the exact equipment to be used.

Are you feeling a strong sense of empathy with this unfortunate student pastor right about now? The point is that technology can be intrusive and when it is, the message gets lost. Each little incident along the road of this Lenten disaster is a lesson on the necessity of proper understanding and skilled application of technology to keep it from undermining or even obliterating the message.

When Technology Is Messianic

"Can you help us out? Almost every church in town has a website except us. If we don't get a website going we're going to miss out on visitors."

The pastor on the other end of the line had a couple of computer savvy people in his congregation who kept asking why their church did not have a website going when most of the other churches had one. He seemed to have a sense that websites held some kind of visitor-generating magic: "Build it (the website), and they will come."

In his book, *The Internet Church*, Walter Wilson writes, "I suggest we as Christians not view the Internet as technology, but as God's moving to bring the gospel to every man, woman, and child upon the earth." He goes on to say at the end of the book that, "With the Internet we have the opportunity to reach every man, woman, and child upon the face of the earth *in the next decade*"[4] (emphasis mine).

Statements like this suggest that having a website is a missional imperative for all churches. The next step in this logic is that *not* having a website is a failure in obedience to the Great Commission. Andrew Carega writes in his book, *eMinistry*, "If the church does not begin to encompass the online world in its ministry, it risks losing even more of its eroding influence in society."[5]

The vision of reaching the entire world for Christ via the Internet in the next decade is exciting. If this could actually be done in ten years, all churches in America should commit every possible dollar to a special outreach offering this coming Sunday. *However . . .* the Internet is *not* a missiological cure-all. In fact, it is a double-edged sword. The Internet indeed has the potential to deliver information concerning the good news of Jesus Christ to almost every person on the planet. At the same time, the Internet can deliver news to everyone on the face of the earth that Elvis Presley is actually Jesus. A search for spiritual truth may lead millions to this news: "Simple and effective Scientology courses, available in missions and churches of Scientology around the world, teach one how to provide practical help—help for life's trials and those daily catastrophes—big and small."[6]

The addition of a website to the local church's ministry will not suddenly produce scores of visitors in worship. The Internet will not automatically generate a worldwide revival of Christianity any more than the Scientology website will produce mass conversion to Scientology. Quentin J. Schultze reflected on this idea in his lecture at the annual meeting of the Internet Evangelism Coalition in Chicago in September of 2002, "Putting the Four Spiritual Laws on four pages of a site will not bring the heathen web-surfing masses to their knees."[7] Instead of persons finding Christ through the Internet, they may simply be using it as an indiscriminate way to fill a spiritual void.

The Internet is aspiritual, areligious, and amoral. In and of itself, the Internet is not a Christian tool any more than it is a Muslim, Hindu, or atheist tool. It is a reflection of the world we live in with all its diversity, beauty, prejudice, sin, and pathology.

Millions of people who journey into cyberspace seeking inspiration or information to fill a spiritual vacuum are not predisposed to seek out Christian websites. In fact, a seeker might stumble onto the Pagan/Wiccan Religion page on the website of About.com. At this site, a former Roman Catholic woman offers advice and counsel.[8] The inquirer can join a discussion on whether one can be a Christian *and* a Wiccan priestess at the same time or purchase a "Retribution Spell" for $19.95 with a "money back guarantee." The visitor to this site is assured: "Spell casting is becoming more and more accepted by mainstream society. And for one simple reason: it works! But only if practiced by someone skilled in the art of spell casting. Our sole mission is to enhance your life—to bring you success, happiness and fulfillment."[9]

Other searchers may come to the website of the Universal Life Church[10] where they can become ordained without cost in minutes and order a "Mini-Clergy Package" (for the new minister) for a mere $14.95. If new ministers want to get their ministry off to a "great start" they can order the "Complete Ministry Package" for $99.95 and receive:

- Their choice of selected honorary doctorate degree
- Their choice of official church title with certificate
- Ordination credential certificate imprinted with their name

- Press pass (blank, with place for your name, address and photo)
- Parking placard for their car windshield
- Deluxe, plastic credit card style wallet credential
- Five certificates of baptism
- Marriage Certificate, Renewal of Marriage, and Affirmation of Love Certificates[11]

Christians may scoff at these sites and their messages, but the point is clear. If the Internet was a missiological silver bullet, the Western world would already be converted to Christianity and the third world would remain largely untouched.

The reality is, however, that some segments of the church are growing rapidly in countries where there are few, if any, technological resources. Yet, the historic mainline denominations in these same locations are in a state of decline. Dennis A. Smith and B. F. Gutierrez (editors) give an account of the phenomenal growth of the Pentecostal church in Latin America to the present time and detail the waning of the mainline church in their book, *In the Power of the Spirit*.[12] Digital technologies have nothing to do with the explosive growth, on the one hand, or decline on the other. Those who believe that the West can win the world, *again*, this time through technological prowess, are wrong. This approach is simply foisting a high-tech version of the same exportation of Western culture upon native cultures that we've seen in the history of missions. The expansion of the indigenous Pentecostal church in Latin America is a strong lesson that growth of the church is based on something more than adding technology to the equation. Obviously the mainline church in Latin America is not in decline because it *lacks* technology any more than the Pentecostal expression of the church *needs* technology to have a vital ministry.

There is a prior spiritual need that is being addressed when vital congregations are growing and thriving. The issue of hunger and malnutrition in our world may provide an analogy for understanding the position of technology in filling this spiritual need. All of us have witnessed countless television reports of famine and starvation all over the third world. Disturbing images of starving men, women, and children have been burned into our minds. I can see very clearly one particular image of a starving child with a distended abdomen who was too weak to brush the flies from her teary eyes. Pictures like this have stirred the hearts of hundreds of thousands who were moved to contribute money for food—hopefully before it was too late. What happens next? All too often, money is collected, food is shipped, and reports surface that the food is sitting in a ship's hold in some harbor, stolen by local bureaucracies or held hostage by political squabbles. Meanwhile, the children continue to die.

To the average person, solving the problem of world hunger should be fairly simple. There is enough food in the world for everyone to have an adequate diet. Why can't we just get the food to those who are dying? It is difficult to accept the fact that the curse of recurring famine and massive starvation of entire populations has to do with personality, politics, greed, and prejudice. The availability of food and the means (technology) to deliver it is not enough to stop the tragedy. There is more to the solution than loading up the family pickup truck and driving off to an encampment of starving people.

Spiritual hunger does not have the direct impact on our senses that physical hunger does. Nevertheless, there are parallels that apply to new technologies and the Internet. People all over the world are malnourished and hungry in a spiritual sense. If spiritual starvation could be portrayed in a physical way, we would be looking at something like the Valley of Dry Bones in Ezekiel's vision (Ezek. 37:1–14). Spiritual starvation leads to spiritual death. And, just as there is an overabundance of physical food that could be given to hungry people, so there is plenty of spiritual food to be had. We also have the technological resources to deliver this food to the world. So, why don't we just ship computers to all the spiritually hungry people, then ship the food (Word of God) via the Internet? As with physical hunger, the reasons why there is spiritual malnutrition and starvation in the world are more complicated than the delivery of food. The proposition that technology somehow holds the answer to the spiritual hunger of millions of people across the world is symptomatic of the spiritual deprivation of the very culture attempting to feed others. Our Western culture is as spiritually lacking as any other, maybe more.

The power of the Internet is phenomenal. But, it is important that we not attribute a messianic quality to a delivery mechanism. Jesus Christ is the food that satisfies spiritual hunger. He says, "I am the living bread that came down from heaven. Whoever eats of this bread will live forever. . . ." (John 6:51). The Internet can be an ally in feeding a spiritually hungry world. It may seem as though we've beaten this dead horse long enough—but trust me. The most common, and perhaps the most dangerous, error I encounter in conferences, classes, and meetings with people who want to use technology in ministry is this mythical notion of the power of the Internet to "change things." Jesus Christ alone can "change things." The Internet cannot. The myth of the magical Internet is not harmless; it leads to a royal waste of time and resources, and it is theologically corrupt. But don't close the book and opt out yet. There is power in the Internet that can be applied in our Christian mission—it is just not *messianic* power. This is good news, because we already have a Messiah.

Lessons from DEN

DEN stands for Digital Entertainment Network (rather—*stood* for). The idea behind DEN was that a full-blown entertainment package would be delivered to the desktops of "Generation Y" (15–25 year olds at the time) and deliver a multi-billion dollar market to investors. In May of 2000, CNET.com carried a story that DEN would file bankruptcy. Giants like Microsoft, Dell Computer, and Chase Capital Partners lost millions.[13]

The amazing thing about this Internet startup was that anyone with a little bit of technological expertise could have told the folks at Ford or Chase Manhattan that the premise of DEN was absolutely faulty. Very simply, there was no infrastructure to carry the services DEN was supposed to deliver. The bandwidth requirements the project demanded were not available in most markets. The magnitude of DEN's claims were not justifiable. Someone with an adequate knowledge of the technology and an understanding of the principles of entertainment could have pointed out the false premise behind DEN's claims.

DEN's CEO, along with the upper echelon of leadership, were in their "twentysomethings" and paid themselves seven-figure salaries. Matt Welch, staff writer and columnist for the Online Journalism Review of Annenberg School for Communication at the University of Southern California, worked briefly for DEN and reported that his annual salary was more than he had earned in his entire life up to that time. When the party was over, 65 million dollars had been invested and wasted. Welch writes that the amazing debacle took place, "because people back then placed monster bets on business buzzwords rather than on the people or products pretending to operate by them. . . . I was fortunate to have the opportunity to see what Rome must have looked like as it burned."[14]

DEN became one of the more spectacular "disappearing wealth" statistics of the dot-com bust. As far removed from the technological efforts of the church as DEN may seem, there are important lessons we need to learn from this, and other, dot-com failures. These lessons can be applied to the use of technology in ministry.

- It is essential to understand the group we propose to reach. "Generation Y" was never likely to center its buying power and entertainment needs in a desktop computer. The church must not buy into the idea that fulfilling community can come through the Internet alone.
- It is essential to be absolutely clear about the message we intend to deliver with our technologies. Congregations do not need more information that reflects the confused and conflicted state of our theological/spiritual foundations.
- It is essential to understand the technology we propose to use. The infrastructure was simply not available to do what DEN proposed to do. *Having* technology does not mean bringing a truckload of computers, LCD projectors, and software to the church office.
- The leadership at DEN did not actually have a plan or principles by which they were going to offer their product. Ministry leaders need to form a coherent plan, propose appropriate programs, and communicate an embraceable vision.
- DEN did not have all the stakeholders on board. Investors, executives, and workers were not together in the mission. It is essential that spiritual leaders work to form the corporation (community) into a team that is supportive of and willing to participate in the mission of the group.

One of the speakers at a ministry and technology conference sponsored by the University of Dubuque Theological Seminary gave a stimulating talk on the use of software in educational ministries. The presentation went well as long as he stayed within his field of expertise.

Unfortunately, as an aside, he suggested that local churches could use an inexpensive digital camera to capture video and webcast the service. He proposed that someone could take a laptop computer to a nursing home, dial up an Internet connection, and show the worship service to someone who was not able to attend worship. "There's no limit to what we can do with technology," he concluded.

The problem is that there actually *is* a limit. A dial-up connection cannot deliver the audio and video data necessary to accomplish a webcast. Internet access is not available in the average nursing home resident's room. It is imperative that we understand the capabilities and limitations of technology so that we do not subvert the realistic gains that can be made. There is a vast array of digital technologies that can be used in ministry. They are really not that difficult to learn, but ministry is best served when teams of trained persons collaborate in the integration of theological understanding and technological delivery.

The good news is that new technologies and the Internet are powerful and useful tools in the delivery of spiritual sustenance to a spiritually hungry world. As long as we understand the potential for regressive use of these tools, we are in a position to move ahead in a positive and informed way.

We will explore the potential of new technologies more fully in the next chapter as we look at how the digital revolution *can*—but does not *necessarily*—lead to the development of authentic community.

The Digitizing of the Church Does Not Necessarily Lead to Development of Community

Communal life is again being recognized by Christians today as the grace that it is, as the extraordinary, the "roses and lilies" of the Christian life.[1]

Dietrich Bonhoeffer

Christian Community Sets the Standard

Before we can discuss how the digital revolution adds to or detracts from Christian community, we need to look at the meaning of community. Dietrich Bonhoeffer's discussion of Christian fellowship in *Life Together* remains one of the more powerful statements of Christian community that has ever been penned outside the New Testament. Although Bonhoeffer's life was cut short by his execution just before

41

the concentration camp at Flossenburg was liberated, his little book remains one of the most popular books in the Christian world.

Bonhoeffer's insistence that Christian community is not the same thing as human fellowship is extremely important for our discussion of the relationship between technology and Christian community.

> Because Christian community is founded solely on Jesus Christ, it is a spiritual and not a human[2] reality. In this it differs absolutely from all other communities. The scriptures call "spiritual" that which is created only by the Holy Spirit, who puts Jesus Christ into our hearts as Lord and Saviour. The scriptures term "human" that which comes from the natural urges, powers, and capacities of the human spirit.[3]

Bonhoeffer's deep commitment to Christian community, born out of his experience with the Confessing Church and its underground seminary, sets the high standard we want to embrace when we assess the value of technological tools in enhancing ministry for the church in our time. The apostle Paul placed the nourishment of the body of Christ at the top of the agenda for Christian leaders: "The gifts he gave were that some would be apostles, some prophets, some evangelists, some pastors and teachers, to equip the saints for the work of ministry, for building up the body of Christ . . ." (Eph. 4:11–12).

We can say with some confidence that authentic leadership in the church brings about a building up of the body of Christ, which, of necessity, includes a deepening of Christian community. Gifted persons who are given to the church by the Spirit of God will minister in a way that draws the community toward its center, namely Jesus Christ. When the community is drawn closer to Christ, the members of the community are brought closer to each other. Notwithstanding, the purpose of this "drawing closer" is not to get closer to the other person, but to Christ. When our intent is to move toward the other person, we are in fact moving away from Christ. If all members of a community are led to Christ, they will find themselves more deeply connected to each other in a spiritual way.

The disciples of Jesus provide an example. In their humanity, they struggled, argued, and found their own community tending toward fragmentation. They were too embarrassed to speak when Jesus asked them why they were arguing with each other as the group journeyed toward Jerusalem. And get this: the dissension took place immediately after the mountaintop of Peter's confession. Jesus had just told them that he would be arrested and executed in Jerusalem. Their response? Mark's Gospel (Mark 9:33–34) tells us they argued with each other about who was the greatest.

Without Christ and his commandment to love each other the way that they were loved by him, there would never have been a Christian community. The death of the leader of this nascent movement would have meant the death of the group. Two things held them together—a commitment to the Christ who was the center of their community and the work of the Holy Spirit who energized them to build up the body of Christ.

In Bonhoeffer's terms, this was a "spiritual" community because it was a community of persons into whose hearts Christ had been placed as Lord and Savior by the work of the Holy Spirit. Apart from this ministry of the Spirit they might have attempted to create a new religious party in the Jewish tradition; they conceivably could have persuaded many that Jesus of Nazareth was the Messiah. But all of this would have been short-lived. The ongoing historical evidence of the reality of the presence of God in the life, mission, and message of Christ has been the persistence of authentic, Spirit-given Christian community.

Success in Building Community—Planning

What does all of this talk about Christian community have to do with ministry and technology? Absolutely everything. If our ministry with all of its technological resources is to bring about the building up of the body of Christ, success will be measured by the quality of Christian community. The deepening of Christian community and the formation of Christian persons require more than enthusiasm for technology.

And there is plenty of enthusiasm to be had. Many are joining the cry. "If you don't get on the digital bandwagon, your church will become irrelevant!" the warning goes. In his introduction to the book *Digital Storytellers* by Len Wilson and Jason Moore, Bill Easum writes, "In the twenty-first century to not be digital will be the new form of illiteracy."[4]

Enthusiasm for technology that does come to fruition in ministry is not new. Consider this evaluation of the use of film in the church: "If they really believe in the promotion of brotherhood, they must seize immediately one of the greatest means to this end. . . ."[5] A former mayor of New Britain, Connecticut, offered to purchase a projector for South Church so that they could illustrate sermons with film.[6] When do you suppose this enthusiasm for the use of technology in ministry took place? Both ideas were part of an article in "The Congregationalist and the Christian World" as far back as July 16, 1910.

Enthusiasm, however, did not get the job done. The potential for community building was lost because of a lack of substantive planning. Besides the barrier of costly projection systems, using Hollywood movies to promote human brotherhood never became mainstream because of the enormous distance between a new technology, a noble idea, and the average congregation. There is always a reality gap between the "latest and greatest" idea and the actual implementation of the idea in the life of the church. Digital technology makes possible the use of sound and image in worship in ways that were never dreamed of just ten years ago. Turning the possibilities into working practice in the mainstream church requires planning. We will explore the issue of planning in more detail in later chapters, but for now it is important to note that Christian community never happens without planning. When using technology in the church it is especially critical that the hard work of planning be engaged.

Success in Building Community—Thinking Theologically

A part of the larger planning task in bringing new technologies into the church is to teach people to think theologically. This is something leaders in the church need to be about in any case, but with technology it is imperative.

For example, a couple of years ago, I worked with a group of people who wanted a website for their church. "We're really blessed," the pastor told me ahead of time, "because one of our deacons is a programmer and another man on the committee has developed a few websites." When we met, I began with a discussion about the purpose for the website, the reasons why the church wanted a website, and how the website would be a part of their overall ministry. A key question in this latter part of the discussion was, "How will this website help in advancing the work of Christ through your church?" After a bit of forced discussion, the programmer-deacon was obviously frustrated and impatient, "Why do we have to do all this theology stuff? Why don't we just get to building the website and let the Christian Education Committee and the pastor discuss these things?"

This man's comment is not so far removed from the mindset of millions of church people all over the country. He is a reflection of a radical wake-up call I experienced in the very first church I served after graduating from seminary. My education prepared me to lead a church that existed in my mind but that was in fact quite different from most mainline churches in America. I had this naïve idea that I was leaving seminary to give leadership to the church of the apostles and martyrs, the legion of dedicated faithful souls whose sole aim in life was to bring the reign of God to a broken world.

At my very first church council meeting, I planned on turning the opening prayer into a short Bible study that would help us as leaders of the church to frame our discussions and decisions in biblical terms. I was naïve enough to believe that the folks on our church council would deeply appreciate my theological insights into our work as a congregation. Indeed, they seemed to listen carefully — not interrupting me even once. After our council meeting, I asked the chairperson for a bit of feedback on our council meeting . . . "especially the Bible study." "Well, pastor," this retired elementary school principal and long-time church worker replied, "I sure do support Bible study, but church council is best suited for taking care of business. We don't have a lot of time for the business of the church and our council members are pretty busy people, you know. We want you to offer that opening prayer, pastor, but the Bible study did take up a lot of time. I'm sure there's plenty of time for the Bible at your Sunday morning adult class." (None of the church council members were in the habit of attending that study.)

This was a wake-up call and the beginning of the transition from theology in the academy to ministry in the real world of parish ministry. After many stumbling steps on my part and with some help from laypeople who were committed to the church, we actually made some gains. With the help of these laypersons we were able to move the church's leadership in the direction of thinking theologically about who we were and what God wanted from us. My initial attempt had been a frontal assault on biblical illiteracy that served only to strengthen the resistance of the council members. Who needs another new pastor fresh out of seminary with the "latest and greatest" way to do church? They had seen it many times, and if the church's leadership was biblically illiterate, the string of newly ordained pastors who quickly moved in and out of this small congregation were contextually illiterate. These pastors may have been theologically correct, but they did not connect with the leaders of the church. The members of the church council, on the other hand, were content to leave biblical theological reflection to the "pros."

As we move into the integration of technology and ministry, it is important to understand that basic principles of successful ministry are not dependent upon the latest and greatest digital tools. Whether it is a new pastor with great promise or new technology with great possibilities, nothing spiritually significant will happen until the people who make up the family of God are *enabled* to think theologically about who they are, what they are called to do, and how each one of them is important to the task.

Success in Building Community—Biblical Foundations

When we examine the meaning of success for the successful integration of technology and ministry, there are important directions to be found in the biblical story. When Joshua found himself leading the entire nation of Israel after the death of Moses it must have been a terrifying experience. The closing words of Deuteronomy tell the tale of a man whose shoes were simply impossible to fill:

> Never since has there arisen a prophet in Israel like Moses, whom the LORD knew face to face. He was unequaled for all the signs and wonders that the LORD sent him to perform in the land of Egypt, against Pharaoh and all his servants and his entire land, and for all the mighty deeds and all the terrifying displays of power that Moses performed in the sight of all Israel. (Deut. 34:10–12)

Frankly, I wouldn't want the job, but it is significant that before Joshua even begins to think about how he will lead this nation, God comes to him with some very specific instructions about what it means to succeed:

> Be strong and courageous; for you shall put this people in possession of the land that I swore to their ancestors to give them. Only be strong and very courageous, being careful to act in accordance with all the law that my servant Moses commanded you; do not turn from it to the right hand or to the left, so that you may be successful wherever you go. This book of the law shall not depart out of your mouth; you shall meditate on it day and night, so that you may be careful to act in accordance with all that is written in it. For then you shall make your way prosperous, and then you shall be successful. (Josh. 1:6–8)

Joshua came to leadership in Israel at a critical time. It was almost a no-win situation for his career. No matter how great Joshua might have been in his leadership, he already knew that he could not measure up to Moses. When it came to miracles, signs, and wonders, he could not even dare to dream his ministry would compare. So how could he be successful?

Take clear notice of God's words to Joshua. He was not to attempt the great miracles of Moses. There was no need to copy Moses' style or imitate his accomplishments. He was simply to give careful attention to the Word of God and to carefully live out its concepts. *Then* he would have success. It would be success in God's way, not in Moses' way, and not even in Joshua's way. It would be God who would be glorified and not Joshua. It was not about numbers; it was not about duplicating someone else's ministry.

Success for Joshua and for everyone since Joshua has been accomplished through faithfulness in context, using the particular skills and tools available at the time. So also the integration of ministry and technology will succeed when the essential aim is to bring glory to God and strength to the church through the particular skills and new tools available in our time.

Three Ministry Principles: Particularity, Intentionality, and Mutuality

Renewal in the church is not a matter of discovering the right program but of engaging in a process. The real need of congregations is for a renewing process rather than a canned renewal program. The *renewing process* is engaged when pastoral leadership and a community of Christian persons join together to engage the ministry principles of particularity, intentionality, and mutuality. From the printing press to television, every advance in technology that brings new possibilities for the church demonstrates the need for ordering principles.

Johannes Gutenberg's moveable type and the printing press brought about a turning point in history, including religious history. The literature of the Protestant Reformation provided the basis for the first technology-driven transformation of the religious landscape. Notice carefully that it was the message that fueled the Reformation, not the printing press in and of itself. The Reformation was a message in search of a tool. Technology is too often a tool in search of a message.

The next major technological revolution to come along was the electronic transmission of data. Progression from the telegraph to television took place in a relatively short period of time historically. Electronic technology held an even greater potential for the Christian world than printing did. Television was not dependent on a literate audience. Radio, television, and film have had an impact on millions of lives, and religious interests have made extensive use of these tools. A case might be made that the electronic age has enabled a transition from the dominance of the mainline church in American life to the emergence of the megachurch and television evangelists. Nevertheless, nothing like the Protestant Reformation has resulted from the electronic age. The essential lesson here is this: It is not technology that finally makes the difference, but the content that is delivered by means of technology. If there is no substance in the website, dazzling technological bells and whistles will not bring return visitors.[7]

Digital technology has placed a powerful tool for ministry at the church's doorstep. If we are to make a successful connection between the emerging digital culture and the Christian community, we will need to have a very clear sense of who we are as "church," what we have been called to do, and how we will go about doing it. Some will miss out on the potential of the new technologies because they embrace technology uncritically and unwittingly embrace the culture that produced the technology. Others will miss the potential because they have opted out of using technology in ministry altogether. In both instances, the potential of digital technology could be realized through application of the ordering principles of particularity, intentionality, and mutuality.

Particularity addresses the question, "Who are we as the people of God?" Our identity as persons is rooted in the life of the God who created us. A sense of living in the presence of God is the basis of particularity for the individual and the community. The author of 1 Peter uses the principle of particularity to encourage a scattered and persecuted people. "But you are a chosen race, a royal priesthood, a dedicated nation and a people claimed by God for his own . . ." (1 Peter 2:9). There are several images in the Bible that provide images of particularity. One church I've studied saw itself as a *journeying people* akin to Moses and the people of Israel looking toward a land of promise. Another congregation saw its life as *living stones* God was using to build a temple. The attempt to integrate new technologies in a church's ministry will fail to build community if it is not rooted in the congregation's understanding of who they are as God's people.

Intentionality moves the principle of particularity into action. Knowing who we are as God's people requires that we faithfully respond to our identity. Intentionality has to do with the expression of who we are in community and in the world. In other words, intentionality has an internal and an external dimension. The internal dimension has to do with *being*, or what we are about in our life together; the external dimension concerns *mission*, or what we are about in the world. Authentic incorporation of technological resources in ministry will facilitate the faithful response of the congregation to an expression of its identity in communal life and mission.

Mutuality has to do with the nature of ministry. Vital churches have a very clear sense of ministry as something that is given to all of God's people. They understand that ministry is an expression of the life of the whole body of Christ and not of one or another individuals in the congregation, ordained or lay. Each congregation in its own way understands the apostle Paul's words in Romans 1:11–12:

> [F]or I long to see you; I want to bring you some spiritual gift to make you strong; or rather, I want to be among you to be myself encouraged by your faith as well as you by mine.

Paul stops in the middle of a sentence to remember the fact that there is a mutuality in the community and in its ministry. Mutuality frees all of God's people for ministry. When technological tools are used in the church's ministry they should not turn most of the congregation into spectators of a tech show, but provide additional opportunities for the ministry of gifted persons.

We need to be aware that technology not only provides new tools for belonging, it also has the potential to draw people into counterfeit community. There is a hunger for authentic connection in our culture, and the Internet has opened up a Pandora's box of opportunity for people to connect with each other. The bad news is that too many of these opportunities hold negative consequences. I want to turn our attention now to the issue of whether the digital world of Generation N is leading to authentic community or a counterfeit collective.

3

The Net Generation (Gen N) — Search for Community

The relentless motion of cyberspace produces an online diaspora, where people experiencing the lightness of digital being gather. Some spend hours online, trying to reach anyone who will care about them, however superficially.[1]

Quentin Schultze

The Great Dis-Connect

One of the central themes of humankind is the dialectical tension between our search for individuality and our search for community. Created as unique, individual children of God, we are nonetheless designed with a deep inner hunger for community. From the very beginning of the biblical drama, God affirmed, "It is not good for the man to be alone . . ." (Gen. 2:18). We were created for fellowship with God and with each other. When we are not connected to God and to others, we are disconnected from God's basic intent for our lives. The classic telling of the story of the original disconnect from God and from each other unfolds in Genesis, when the man and woman take matters into their own hands, choose their own wisdom over God's, and become separated from God and from each other. Instead of the immediate communion they had with God, there was an inner homesickness. The intimate relationship between the man and woman was replaced by shame, suspicion, and blame. Instead of being transparent to each other, they desired to hide. They experienced a need to cover themselves, and in their hiding from God, they irreparably damaged their relationship with each other.

A wistful longing now pervades the human spirit because of this disconnect, which is at the heart of the human condition. A driving inner tension we might call the original "hide and seek" syndrome governs our inner life. We want to hide even as we want to belong.

The Digital Tools of Gen N

Gen N does not have a greater need than any other generation for belonging, but they do have a multitude of digital tools with which to engage their search. They have ways to connect that are beyond the wildest fictions of their elders' youthful days. Remember Dick Tracy's two-way wrist radio? Don't feel badly if you don't—those of us who remember Dick Tracy are a shrinking minority. Dick Tracy was the name of a comic strip authored by Chester Gould for forty-six years, beginning in 1931. Tracy fought the forces of evil with his incredible two-way wrist radio. The *Augusta Chronicle*, in its online column, tells the story of the beginning of Tracy's new "gizmo gadget." "When Tracy first cocked his arm and summoned the police dispatcher Jan. 13, 1946, the otherwise terse detective filled the airwaves with a euphoric chatter exceeding anything he uttered to his longtime love, Tess Trueheart. 'It's the most remarkable invention of its age,' Tracy gushed. 'It's miraculous. It both sends and receives!'"[2]

Dick Tracy, eat your heart out. The tools Gen N consider essential for daily living go beyond anything even Chester Gould could ever have imagined. The program assistant for our seminary technology department is right at the leading edge of Gen N (anyone born since

1977). Here is her list of absolutely essential, must-have tools for everyday living.

Cell phone (Which is also her alarm clock, address book, calculator, Internet access when on the road, and mobile instant messenger.)

Computers (Desktop and laptop—it is not acceptable to have only one computer. Her household has three computer users and thus requires one desktop for each user and a home network for resource sharing.)

IM (Instant messaging. Absolutely essential software which allows instant, always-on contact with friends, family, and coworkers. Gen N can communicate with five, six, or even ten people at once.)

DVD Player (One in the desktop and one in the laptop. The laptop DVD can be connected to the TV.)

MP3 Player (I asked her if a "boom box" was a necessary item. She responded, "That is so ten years ago!")

ISP (Internet Service Provider, to access the Internet and provide space for a personal Web page. Of course, everyone should have a Web page!)

Digital Voice Recorder (Allows direct download to a laptop computer.)

PDA (Palm Pilot, Handspring, or other personal digital assistant.)

GPS (Global positioning system, to call a service like Northstar and get directions to anywhere at anytime. Really necessary for a woman traveling alone.)

Digital Cameras (One for still photography and one digital camcorder.)

Gizmo Gadgets (Quoting Dick Tracy. Nice-to-have entertainment items. These include Play Station, Microsoft Xbox, or other video game players. Although not a need for our program assistant, some young folk would consider lack of a game pass to online games a form of deprivation. Apple iPod, the upscale MP3 player—iPod's 20 GB model can hold 4,000 songs.)

One of the differences between Gen N and the rest of us is that they have grown up with a language we have to learn. MP3, ISP, PDA, and IM are all common vocabulary for them. If you already own the

digital devices and understand the language, you have the technological prerequisites to be a strong candidate for youth leader in most
congregations.

On the other hand, the older generations have a language Gen N is
not familiar with. I was trying to talk my eight-year-old daughter into
surrendering some computer time on our new iMac. I explained that I
had a lot of work to do at home because of a network upgrade that was
going on at the University. I tried for a little sympathy by explaining
to her that the computers at my office might not be working and that
I might even have to use a typewriter at work the next day. She gave
me the most quizzical look and asked, "What is a typewriter?" When I
explained the typewriter to her (my once state-of-the-art IBM Selectric),
she got up from the iMac and said simply, "I don't think I would like
a typewriter."

The cell phone is no longer just a convenient addition to the regular family phone. For most younger folks, a cell phone is the primary
phone. Many do not have a wired phone at all. Wireless is the norm,
and nobody is at home anyway. This is the world of mlife, which is
AT&T's version of mobile communication services. Their slogan says
it all, "Welcome to mlife . . . it's your life made truly mobile."[3] Based
on GPRS (general packet radio service) technology, the mobile phone
can now deliver voice and data with an "always on" connection to
the Internet. The phone can come with a joystick for "gamers" and
an optional snap-on MP3 player and digital camera. High-end users
can snap a picture and send it to a friend's phone or PC or store it in
a photo album. If someone should happen upon a newsworthy event,
they could snap a photo and send it to the newsroom of their local
newspaper or television station. When this mobile phone rings, it is
possible to see who is calling through a digital photo that pops up in
caller ID. A friend can be brought into a three-way call in which the
group can check what movies are playing, find a local restaurant, get
directions to where they want to go with GPS, and arrange the evening's
activities. The portable phone of fifteen years ago has evolved into a
cell phone that is now a "must have" connectivity tool, especially for
Gen N. A new service allows persons to turn on their cell phone, make
themselves "visible" to others who have their phones turned on, and
locate up to five friends at once.

Remember the old question, "What will they think of next?" That's almost irrelevant for Gen N. Everybody knows "they" are not only thinking, they are rolling out new products and innovations faster than any one person can keep track of. You don't have to wonder what they will think of next, you will likely trip over it in your daily living. Gen N has more digital tools available for getting connected and staying connected than any generation to date has even dreamed of. I can recall my parents insisting that I "quit tying up the phone line" when I was talking with friends. The phone was our tool for connectivity. There was a beginning to the connection when we dialed a number (not pushed, mind you, but dialed) and an end to the connection when we hung up the phone. There was no "always-on" connectivity. For us, it took a little effort to "connect." But for Gen N, the effort comes in "disconnecting."

Digital tools for a digital world and virtual connections in a virtual world are the stuff of Gen N. Is all this bringing about genuine community and a sense of belonging in terms of authentic Christian connections? The lines have begun to blur between the real world filled with digital tools and the virtual world created with digital tools. There is a price to pay for all this connectivity. It is critical to raise the question as to whether Gen N's digital world is facilitating true belonging or drawing them into a false sense of community. The virtual communities many people, especially Gen N, participate in cannot lessen the deep-seated disconnect of life without God.

The Digital World of Generation N

Dubuque Theological Seminary offers technology training conferences for Christian leaders. A group of leaders at one of our technology conferences was having a discussion about youth ministry during a coffee break. One of the participants was a pastor who is very up to date on things technological and an evangelist for the use of technology in the church. He observed, "The churches in my area are missing the boat with Gen N."

"What in the world is 'Gen N'?" a woman asks.

The pastor continued, "Gen N is short for the term 'Net Generation' and includes everyone who was born after about 1977. These kids have no idea what a world without the Internet or digital media is like."

The woman responded by expressing her frustration with yet another way the church gets divided into groups, "Not another generation something. It seems as though people are always coming up with ways to divide people, especially in the church. There's the Senior Group, the Couple's Club, the Singles Group, the Youth Group, and then all this generation stuff came along. Baby Boomers, Baby Busters, the Me Generation, Generation X. Now a Generation N?"

A lively discussion followed as to whether the digital revolution means there is something unique about children and young people who have never experienced a world without the Internet and digital media. I can understand the frustration. It is still difficult for me to grasp the fact that my eight-year-old daughter can be out in cyberspace while she is sitting in the same room as I am. I have to consciously remind myself that she is visiting a world "out there somewhere," even though we are physically together in the seeming safety of our home. I am a part of the analog generation. She is Gen N; she has never been anything but digital. For instance, there was the day she stood amazed when her mother was looking for a particular song on an audio cassette tape. Of course, the right spot was not easy to find. As her mother hit rewind then fast forward a few times, my daughter asked, "Why didn't you get a CD?"

There is no doubt that digital technologies have had an impact on the family, social, and educational lives of young people. But is all this technology good for our children? Is it doing something bad to them we older folk can't quite discern? Are they weird as well as wired, and is it the wired part that has the potential to make them weird? How worried should we be?

Don Tapscott, in his book *Growing Up Digital: The Rise of the Net Generation*, calls these young people "N-Geners," and he is optimistic about their digital world. "Everybody relax. The kids are all right. They are learning, developing and thriving in the digital world. . . . What we know for certain is that children without access to the new media will be developmentally disadvantaged." Tapscott acknowledges that there are many issues that need to be addressed with the introduction of digital technologies in the lives of Generation N, but mostly, he sees the adult world as needing to change. "Rather than hostility and mistrust on the part of adults, we need a change in thinking and in behavior on the part of parents, educators, lawmakers, and business leaders alike."[4]

Tapscott's view is somewhat naïve in its optimism about the basic goodness of the digital world our young people dwell in. Nevertheless, he is correct in his assessment of the need for the adult world to make some changes. This is especially true in the church. We need to realize that the genie is out of the bottle and that there are bad things as well as good things in this digital world. We church leaders need to be literate in digital technologies and open to innovation if we are to have credibility with a growing segment of the church.

The Vulnerability of Gen N

There is a special way in which Gen N is at risk in the digital world. This is especially true for adolescents and preadolescents. They are technologically savvy, and at the same time, they are emotionally vulnerable. During a time of life when they are experiencing the chaos of identity formation most forcibly and testing out who they are in the crucible of family life, they are searching for meaning and connection. One of the ways life is different in our digital world is the fact that much of this searching is accomplished in a virtual world. There is no time other than adolescence when the questions "Who am I?" and "Do I belong?" are more critical. Tragic stories of cyber predators lurking in chat rooms have grown at an alarming rate over the past few years. These predators hide behind a mask of caring, compassion, and understanding as they draw children into their twisted worlds.

A dramatic portrayal of cyber predators is a 1998 made-for-cable movie starring Cheryl Ladd, *Every Mother's Worst Fear.* The movie addresses the worst fears of any parent whose child spends time on the Internet. The story is supposedly inspired by actual events. Unfortunately the film panders to the rampant technophobia of uninformed parents, but the basic message is important. The story involves the predictable plot of a teenage girl, Martha, who participates in a chat room and falls prey to a cyber predator. The girl lives with her divorced mother who spends lots of time at her career and not as much time with her daughter. Martha is lonely and vulnerable and agrees to meet the cyber predator in a hotel room, where she is kidnapped and forced into the world of cyber porn. Her plight seems hopeless when an escape attempt is thwarted. With hopeless tears she sobs, "How did you find me?" He answers, "I found you because you wanted to be found." Martha had simply longed to be listened to and cared for, and the virtual perfect man was just on the other side of her computer screen. When the crisis is finally resolved and, against all odds, Martha is reunited with her mother, she says, "Mom, there are some things I haven't told you." This, of course, is not news to mom, who replies, "There is nothing you could ever do that would make me stop loving you. You know that, don't you?"

This is the central affirmation every human being needs and longs to hear. When this longing is not addressed, people consciously or unconsciously enter a desperate search for community. This is true for our grandfather's generation as well as for Gen N. Everyone needs to hear this affirmation in order to gain a sense of belonging. Within the safety of this belonging, persons develop the trust and confidence needed to come out of hiding. Behind the scenes and between the lines of our living is the quest to reconnect with the absolute, unconditional love of God and with a community of other persons. It is the most natural thing of all that at the heart of Gen N's desire to be plugged in is the need to belong and the need to be loved. The vulnerability of a child (or of any of us for that matter) is inversely proportional to the strength of the love and belonging they experience in their primary social environment.

Deficient Connections—The "Virtual Collective"

People whose primary communities are Internet-based are attempting to fulfill a need for genuine community through what I call a "virtual collective." This virtual collective is a phantom community, a digital masquerade of real community. The virtual collective seems to fill a need for community, but in fact misses the mark.

Most of us do not like being lonely, and N-Geners hate it. I've asked a few N-Geners what it would be like if they woke up and their cell phone, computer, instant messaging, and other digital gadgets were all gone. The response is almost always a tortured expression that betrays an intense inner conflict. I can hear the wheels turning, "Aaarrgh! What is life without my digital connectivity?" An example is the time one of our babysitters was telling us that she was grounded for ten days for breaking curfew. We asked how it was going and she said, "No problem, I've got my cell phone and my computer, so it's cool." In the "olden days" grounding meant being cut off from one's community of friends. Our sitter was grounded, but she never missed a beat in being connected to her friends. Perhaps contemporary grounding should not be a physical thing. When someone is grounded, maybe we take away their cell phone and turn off their IM.

The question that begs asking in Gen N's world is whether the community that results from this plethora of digital tools is authentic community in a Christian sense, as we have been discussing it, or a kind of assimilation into a virtual collective. One way to understand the subtle power of the virtual collective is to examine MMORPGs (massively multiplayer online role-playing games). In these games, hundreds and even thousands of players go online to explore worlds, engage in battle, and hunt down prey.

The most striking example is the game *Everquest* (EQ), which has approximately 400,000 players worldwide. The game allows people to interact with others in a virtual world. They choose and develop characters, pick a community in which to live, join a guild, and go on team adventures. Information about EQ and other RPGs (role-playing games) that would be helpful for parents and Christian leaders can be found at the MMORPG Café website.[5] The game is so addictive that even the most devoted players jokingly refer to *Everquest* as "Evercrack," CBS correspondent Jon Frankel reported.[6] People can get totally lost in the *Everquest* version of this particular virtual collective. Marriages have ended, relationships have been broken, and one mother blames *Everquest* for her son's suicide.[7] Shawn Wooley, the young man who committed suicide, spent up to twelve hours a day logged on to EQ for over a year. Wooley's mother said, ". . . he logged into the game and logged out of his life. . . . He stopped trying because it was easier to move on in the game than it was in real life. . . . The last time he logged onto *Everquest* was 6 A.M. Someone heard the shot around 11. When I found him he was sitting at the computer with *Everquest* on and that's where he killed himself."[8]

Why Virtual Communities Miss the Mark

Admittedly, people whose lives are damaged by addiction to an online game, and especially the horrible consequences that came to the Wooley family, are not the norm for N-Geners. There is tension between the

Sony corporation, owners of EQ, and individuals who want warnings and even policing on the part of game creators, but in the end Scott McDaniel, vice president of Sony Online Entertainment, has it right. "It's not our job to police how long people are playing in our virtual world; it's really up to the individual to make sure they are not taking it too far."[9] Many of us may not want to hear it, but it is not the responsibility of New York, Hollywood, or the Silicon Valley to ensure the responsible use of entertainment modalities or digital technologies.

It is, however, the responsibility of the people of God to understand the world of Gen N and aggressively pursue the missional responsibility of the church to reach "the ends of the earth." This imperative is no less applicable to the world of Shawn Wooley or Gen N than it is to any other segment of God's children. Thousands of young and not so young people find their lives devoid of meaning to the point that they build alternative identities in cyberspace. Knowing who we are and developing our sense of self is a monumental task for every child and adolescent. The particular danger of sophisticated MMORPGs is that an actual virtual world exists that can turn a face-to-face relationship into face-to-back-of-the-head-at-a-computer relationship. People who are trapped in lives of painful existence, whether of their own making or not, are extremely vulnerable to the appeal of a virtual world where they can try on new personalities and engage in challenging adventure.

The more extreme experiences of the most perilous MMORPGs do not represent the majority of online communities, but all online communities are fundamentally flawed in terms of delivering valid Christian community. Virtual communities cannot provide or replace Christian community for several reasons.

- Virtual community is community without accountability. People can log on whenever they wish, participate as they feel the need, and say whatever they wish. This venue, which has been called the ultimate democratic medium, is also a chaotic medium where no one is accountable. It is not possible to mature in an environment without accountability.
- Virtual community does not have canons of truth. It is easy to deceive and be deceived in virtual communities. Identities are unchecked, and in spite of all the family-oriented filters and web-

site blocking software available, there is no truth filter. That leaves many people extremely vulnerable. Without truth, there is no real freedom.

- Virtual community does not have permanence. If there is any place in our culture where people are "here today and gone tomorrow," it is in the virtual world. Everyone who uses e-mail knows the meaning of "User Unknown." Virtual soul mates can disappear in the blink of an eye or the click of a mouse. Without the presence of other persons, it is not possible to be encouraged on the way toward maturity.

- Virtual community does not have "real presence." For Christian people, the incarnation is fundamental to who we are as persons and who we are as a community. We are not simply a gathering of persons, but the community of redeemed persons. Christ, our Emmanuel, is "God with us." In the community of faith we are present to and with each other and Emmanuel binds us together. Christian persons may use online connections to facilitate community, but that community cannot exist without the community of "real presence" where real people gather as the body of Christ.

In spite of all the tools available for connecting with friends and engaging in online community, the result has not been the discovery of authentic community, but a blurring of the lines between virtual and real living. The suicide of Shawn Wooley is an extreme example, but there are hundreds of thousands of N-Geners who have a symbiotic relationship with virtual collectives. Without the characteristics of accountability, truth, permanence, and presence, they find the lines between themselves and the collective blurred.

The church is failing to reach out to Gen N on two fronts. In the first instance, there is a tendency to embrace digital technologies without theological-spiritual discernment. The sense is that if we create enough websites, open up enough Christian chat rooms, and put enough copies of the Four Spiritual Laws out in cyberspace, we will win the world, and especially Gen N, for Christ. It is not that we should be absent from these things, but that we ought not think that these efforts alone will qualify for the Master's, "Well done, thou good and faithful servant . . ." (Matt. 25:21 KJV).

In the second instance there is the easy out that sees the Internet as a tool of the devil. If this is all of Satan, then there is no need to do the hard work of working for spiritual, theological integrity in the use of technology for ministry. Another failure of the church might be phrased, "the mainline is the sideline." It is no secret that the mainline church seriously lags behind the rest of the world in using technology for the missional imperative of Christian faith. While often critical of some of the more sophisticated technological savvy of the evangelical church, the mainline church has largely ignored the great potential of technology to reach out to Gen N. No church in America should hire a youth pastor or youth director who is not literate with current technologies. Failure to engage the digital world of Gen N is to turn away from a huge segment of our contemporary culture.

Connecting in the Christian Community

We need to explore a bit further how Christian community provides a foundation from which online experience can be profitable. Authentic Christian community is essential to integrating technology and ministry in a disconnected world. In Christian community, there is an opportunity to work out the strange contradictions that come from our human desire to hide and yet to belong. This is not always an easy task, but it is a workable one because Christian people who are bound together in community at the very least affirm mutual commitments. We Christians do not always get it right, but we are bound to the basic premise that Jesus Christ is Lord. The book of the prophet Isaiah gives a name to the disconnect between God and humanity, ". . . your iniquities have been barriers between you and your God, and your sins have hidden his face from you so that he does not hear" (Isa. 59:2).

The essential core of God's redemptive plan is that Christ comes to take upon himself the consequences of human failure and willingly plumbs the depths of separation from God. One of the best known events in all of Scripture is Jesus' cry from the cross, "My God, my God, why have you forsaken me?" (Mark 15:34). The crux of redemption is Jesus' entering into and emerging from a sense of absolute separation from God. This act makes it possible to reconnect with the Source of authentic life. In Christian terms, the great disconnect is a result of sin, and reconnection is made possible in Christ. God's redemptive action in Christ and the incorporation of redeemed persons in the community of faith, or the unity of trinity in community, becomes the absolute foundation of community in the company of the redeemed.

I submit that a Christian doctrine of sin — properly taught — can supply the necessary correction to a naïve baptism of technology as God's great new gift for ministry. Understanding sin as endemic to humanity can dispel the myth that an indiscriminate integration of technology is an effective means of ministry. The presence of cyber stalkers in the online world demonstrates that sin is no respecter of persons. Every tool for good will find its way into the hands of saints or sinners without prejudice. It is not the tool, but the hand that wields it, that makes the difference in advancing or corrupting the kingdom of God. St. Francis's words, "Lord make me an instrument of thy peace," point to the foundational premise of ministry and technology. The thing that is being used along with the person who uses it can only advance the kingdom of God when fully given into the hands of God.

Working with digital technologies in order to reach out to Gen N has no shortcuts. Technology in and of itself is not able to bring about authentic community for a generation that has no idea what a world without the Internet is like. It does, however, provide significant new tools. Caring persons who are spiritually connected with God, grounded in the community of the redeemed, and skilled in the use of digital technologies have great potential for ministry in a disconnected world.

Before we move on to explore the promise of digital technologies, we need to consider one last peril of technology that could sideline the effort to help people discover authentic connection and belonging.

Reflections
of Our Digital Culture
in the Church

A Chronic State of Alarm

VCR is blinking 12:00. The kids are doing their homework by e-mail. Your pager beeps as the cell phone rings. . . . You are lost without the schedule in your personal data assistant. The fax machine is out of paper, the photocopier is jammed, and you just spilled coffee over everything when you tripped over the scanner's cables. . . . Thank heavens your job is made easier by all this![1]

John Mueller

Four simple words can strike terror into the hearts of thousands of people around the world at any given moment. "The system is down!" There are variations like "The network is down" or

"The Internet is down," but the result is always the same. Blood pressure rises, hearts begin to pound, and people frantically set about trying to correct whatever it is that is bringing their world to a screeching halt.

I know, I've been there. I have preached sermons to myself about the dangers of being outer-directed by technological crisis instead of inner-directed by faith and trust. Nevertheless I have found myself squarely in the custody of a tech crisis on more than one occasion. A vivid example is one day a little over a year ago when twenty people from several states had gathered at the University of Dubuque to be trained in using our online learning system. A trainer was flown in from Washington, D.C., schedules had been manipulated for weeks, and events had been cancelled just to get this one day of training put together—training that was highly dependent on access to the Internet. The day arrived, all participants were settled into their workstations in our finest computer lab, the instructor began by introducing herself, and it was time for that great sigh of relief. It was going to be a great day for the program.

At this point, the face of our microcomputer specialist appeared in the small window of the door to the lab. His finger beckoned me into the hallway. "This is not going to be good news," I thought. People in tech support do not call program directors into the hall to say, "Have a nice day." I quietly left the computer classroom with a sense of dread that was quickly confirmed. "The Internet is down!" His words triggered a roller coaster ride as I went from sigh of relief to state of alarm.

A Chronic State of Alarm

Psychologist Walter B. Cannon coined the phrase "Fight or flight"[2] in 1914. Cannon's work explored the results of long-term stress on physical well-being. When we experience stress, our bodies react with a rush of chemicals that prepare us for combat or flight. Hans Selye, an Austrian-born physician, more than any other researcher continued Cannon's work and demonstrated that stress is an exceptionally powerful influence on our lives.[3] When our microcomputer specialist support shattered the vision of an uneventful day of training with the words, "The Internet is down," I became a classic example of Cannon's fight or flight. My heart began to race, my breathing became more shallow, my pupils dilated, and tension ran through my body. I was ready to smash my computer (fight) or run away (flight). The problem is that there is no physical fight that ensues or race that is run. The body gets ready to exert itself, and the energy rush is trapped. Eventually we are stressed out.

One real problem with contemporary technology is that it keeps us in this chronic state of alarm. People who work with technology are particularly susceptible to this "always-on" alarm. This has not changed in the thirty-six years I have been involved with technology. Whether it was the accounting program that would not work at IBM's Service Bureau Corporation in 1968 or an upgrade that did not get done in time in 2002, the proverbial light at the end of the tunnel is indeed a freight train. There is always a hope that when the next upgrade is completed, the current network disruption figured out, the latest computer configured, or the new server installed, we will be able to slow down and relax a bit. But the slowdown never comes. It is a wishful dream that haunts tech people who dwell in a land of persistent crisis.

Another technology that has the potential to really run amuck is e-mail. A few years ago, we were asking friends, neighbors, pastors, and churches to get e-mail. How much simpler it is to e-mail bulletin information to the church secretary, send pictures of the youth group to the newsletter editor, or get a message to the pastor just before you retire for the evening knowing she will get your message as soon as she signs on to her computer. You have likely seen the commercial where the computer is turned on and a "hard-to-believe-it's-a-computer" voice softly intones, "You've got mail." However, many people are discovering that e-mail can be a real hassle. It is not uncommon for people to spend up to an hour each day just sorting through their e-mail at work. I personally find e-mail overwhelming on some days and have set some limits for my online students about just how much e-mail I will allow to be stuffed into my inbox.

E-mail comes with the implication that because a message can be transmitted instantly, it should somehow be answered instantly. A few years ago I was urging members of the congregation I was serving to get e-mail. "We could improve communication in the church in a wonderful way if more people just had e-mail," I said on more than one occasion. Soon the congregation had scores of people with e-mail. Within twelve months of this big push, I was asking, "What was I thinking?" More than once, someone would send an e-mail with a question or request and a second within thirty minutes saying something like: "Pastor, I sent an e-mail to you and have not heard back yet." In this age of instant gratification, e-mail can be just one more thing in our lives that demands immediate response.

Technolust and the Increase of Urgency

Technology has infiltrated large parts of our lives and created a "have to" mentality. That which is possible becomes that which is pressing. Things we *can* do gradually turn into things we *must* do. When we walk in the door, we have to see if there is e-mail waiting, and if there is, we have to read it right away. When we leave home, we have to take the cell phone, and if it rings, we have to answer it. Ann Barbour in the *Online Observer* writes about people who have cell phones plastered to their heads, ". . . even getting groceries? My God, who do you need to talk to when you are getting groceries? Make a list."[4]

The urgency of the technological in our lives is complicated by what can be best described as "Technolust." A list of the things most people consider necessities will generate items unheard of ten years ago. Instead of bringing the anticipated convenience and ease to living, our technological paraphernalia has come with significantly increased demands on our time and energy. There is a subtle downward spiral whereby more technology becomes less quality of life. More technology equals more work. The computers, VCRs, cell phones, digital TV, cable access, microwave ovens, and a plethora of remote control devices have transformed leisure time into work time and family time into individual time. There is a fragmentation that takes place when all members of the family have their own communication and entertainment devices. Each one of these devices contributes another possibility for urgency to invade everyday life. Who among us has not heard the pitiful wailings of a teenager who has lost her cell phone or a "couch-potato" husband who cannot find the TV remote?

Where is the promised respite that these tools and toys were supposed to bring? Respite is a central biblical theme. Respite is rest and rest is sabbath: ". . . a sabbath rest still remains for the people of God; for those who enter God's rest also cease from their labors as God did from his" (Heb. 4:9–10). Quentin Schultze observes that, "Information technologies are not just tools, but also value laden techniques that we rely on increasingly to organize and understand nearly every aspect of our lives."[5] Insofar as technology removes sabbath from our lives, it represents a toxic influence in our spirituality.

It is critical for the relationship between ministry and technology that core values of the Christian community are not subverted by a false assumption that technology is a gift from God that can be uncritically imported into the life of the church. Technology's increasing grip on our individual and corporate lives is too easily transferred to technology in the church. The lust for all the latest and greatest "gizmo-gadgets" can foist its noxious imperatives on our ministry. Beware of these imperatives, "We have to have it," "It has to work," and "It has to work now!" This sense of urgency has invaded our work lives, our family lives, and has the potential to negatively impact our lives as the people of God. When we import technology into the life of the church without discernment, we also import the chronic state of alarm that plagues technology.

The Myth of Christian Computing

One example of how the church is vulnerable to the technological tyranny of the urgent is this statement from an ad on the *Christian Computing Magazine* website. The ad is for a videotape called *How to Use the Internet to Grow Your Church*. It reads, "Statistics show that if churches do not begin to better use the Internet to reach their communities, as well as provide ministry opportunities for their members, they will decline."[6]

Frankly, the majority of declining churches would do well to forget the Internet and technology and focus their efforts on building community, doing evangelism, and encouraging Bible study. Technology will not reverse the fortunes of churches that are in a state of decline. Reasons for the decline are myriad, but the lack of Internet usage is not one of them. Otherwise, one might safely assume that all churches began seeing great increases in the mid-1990s.

We need to be careful of the terms we use when we make use of technology. "Christian computing" is a myth. When the term "Christian" is used as an adjective to describe commercial products, the word Christian is trivialized. A "Christian" something or other is more often a marketing ploy than it is a spiritual or theological commitment. A search of the Internet using "Christian" as an adjective produces an incredible number of "hits." The search term "Christian computers" yields websites such as christianchurchstore.com and christiancom puterstore.com. You can buy computers through these websites, but the computers all have motherboards, memory, keyboards, and monitors like any "pagan" computer. The merchandise is no less expensive than computers at any other online store.

Anyone can launch a website, sell computers and peripherals through PCMall or a number of other online stores, and name the site "Joe's Christian Technology Store." Other searches that produce thousands of results are "Christian dating," "Christian chat rooms," "Christian travel," and a personal favorite, "Christian promotions." The latter will take you to online stores where you can buy tote bags, vinyl stickers, car and truck door magnets, coffee mugs, bumper stickers, and even napkins—all qualifying for the description "Christian."

The attempt to define Christian computing is as silly as defining a Christian bumper sticker. Follow along as I imagine with you what Christian computing might be all about: If a Christian is doing Christian computing and along the way becomes a heretic, is he no longer doing Christian computing? And if he happened to buy a Christian computer through an online Christian computer store, would the computer still be a Christian computer? Or does it inherit the shame of the heretic and become a secular computer? Hopefully, you get the idea that Christian computing is a myth.

Bill Gates Wants a Voice in Your Church

In the last chapter, I mentioned that one of the ways the church is failing to reach out to Gen N comes from those who see the Internet as an instrument of the devil. A small but noisy group portrays Bill Gates as the personification of evil. These modern Luddites[7] raise their own version of a chronic state of alarm as they go about warning us about the evils of the Internet and Bill Gates.

Bill Gates is the public face of Microsoft corporation and the con-summate example of *Revenge of the Nerds* in modern history. Microsoft shot into the commercial sky like a rocket in the last two decades of the twentieth century. When personal computing was young and the

Internet was brand new and unknown, Christians were exceptionally distrustful of this new technology. "I think the Internet is an instrument of the devil," one woman said to me in the mid-nineties. Not only was the Internet suspect, but Bill Gates himself was seen by some as the Antichrist. My parishioner bought into this.

The notion that Bill Gates is the Antichrist has been circulated by e-mail and posted on hundreds of websites for years. There was a flurry of e-mail in 1998 that came with the appeal, ". . . please share this to all your friends with or without e-mail . . ." and included something like this, "Do you know that Bill Gates' real name is William Henry Gates III? His official real name now is Bill Gates III. So what's so eerie about this name? Ok, if you take all the letters in Bill Gates III and then convert it in ASCII code (American Standard Code for Information and Interchange) and then add up all the numbers you will get 666 which is the number of the beast!!! Sick!!! Coincidence huh? Nope. Take Windows 95 and do the same procedure and you will get 666, too! And the same goes for MS-DOS 6.31!"[8]

There is no denying the fact that Bill Gates is wealthy and that Microsoft has become a prosperous and powerful corporation. But to be realistic, Microsoft does not hold a candle to the oil giants or the automobile industry. In fact, in *Fortune 500's* 2003 ranking of corporate revenues, Microsoft's revenue was only 11 percent of Wal-Mart's. It was a rough year for technology companies when these statistics were gathered, but even the troubled airline industry giant Boeing bested Microsoft by more than 100 percent. Microsoft Corporation revenues came in number 47 out of the top 100 corporations.[9]

Does Bill Gates want a voice in your church? Insofar as by Bill Gates we mean Microsoft Corporation, of course it wants a voice in your church. But so does Wal-Mart, Dell Computer, K-Mart, or State Farm Insurance for that matter—all of whom fared better than Microsoft in *Fortune's* top 100 list for 2002. This is not a matter of a conspiracy or sinister plot to take over the church. As the corporate world knows, "It's the economy stupid!" There is nothing new about corporations wanting all the possible revenue they can generate, and the wider church is a significant consumer in the contemporary market place. The church needs insurance coverage and supplies for the office, kitchen, and Sunday school. It also needs computers in a world that has been changed forever by the digital revolution. It is because the digital technologies are new and mysterious that sinister myths about companies like Microsoft and persons like Bill Gates are generated. Because the technology is new and scary for many people, the world of digital technology seems to threaten a hostile takeover of the kingdom of God. I suppose there is someone somewhere who might think Sam Walton is an enemy of the kingdom or agent of evil, but for most of us, Wal-Mart is just "plain folks" like you and me who sell all the things we need under one roof. The voice Bill Gates or Microsoft wants in your church is not a sinister plot from the pits of hell. Like everyone else who sells something, Microsoft wants you to buy their products.

Hurry-Up Sickness—The Rush to Mediocrity

The church is extremely vulnerable to one particular aspect of the chronic state of alarm that plagues the world of technology, namely "hurry-up sickness." Digital technology has made it possible for the church to worship, learn, and reach out in powerful new ways. Worship can include film clips, PowerPoint[10] presentations, and movies created by the youth group. Scores of new websites are launched by churches on a daily basis with the expectation of reaching whole communities. Bible studies can be conducted online, and literally every group in the church can have its own online community. Thousands of churches are already doing these things, and thousands more just can't wait to get on board. And the vast majority of them will do it poorly! The rush to implement the possibilities of digital technology in our work as God's people is a rush to mediocrity; God is not calling us to mediocre ministry.

The church has not escaped the panicky, hurry-up sickness of the world it lives in. We want more members, more money, bigger buildings, and a big technology budget. And we want it now. "There's a lot of competition out there," one church leader said to me as we were discussing the struggling small church he belonged to. "We've got to do something, anything, quickly if we are going to survive!" he said.

Let me promise you, technology will not save your struggling or dying church! Strong, discerning leadership, along with committed, growing Christians is what it takes to work for the kingdom of God. Technology can be a wonderful tool and a powerful ally in the effort to build the kingdom, and we will move on to that in the next section of this book. The task in this first part of the book has been to reflect on the pitfalls that beset the church in its initial encounters with new technologies. There is so much promise in digital technology if we will just step back, take a deep breath, and carefully consider the possibilities.

Part 2

Develop Knowledge of the Promise

Forget About Technology— But If You Must— And We Know You Will

New Directions and Opportunities

A computer alone will not help you solve life's problems, save you money, or help you relate to others better. . . . I have a love/hate relationship with computers, and although I rely on them, I'm waiting for the next major solar flare to wipe them all out.[1]

I-Hate-Computers.org

When you begin to integrate new technologies into ministry, it will be necessary to successfully navigate the minefield of dangerous pitfalls, some of which have been discussed in Part 1 of this book. In fact, perhaps you might be better off forgetting about technology. The problem with this is that none of us can really forget about technology. It is a virtual elephant that dwells even in the living rooms of those who still hold out for life without digital technology. There is, however, a legitimate decision to be made with respect to whether the engagement with technology will be nominal or dynamic.

Nominal engagement means that a church or Christian leader decides to make use of the advantages of a cell phone, office computers, printers, fax machines, and other digital equipment without bringing technology into areas of education, worship, and evangelism. There are no plans for a website, purchase of an LCD projector, or Power-Point presentations and movie clips in worship. This could be a very good technology decision based on leadership, ministry, or economic factors. I want to press for the position, however, that this should be a conscious, informed decision on the part of the congregation or ministry's leadership. Nominal engagement with technology means that questions were raised and answers reached. It is not merely defaulting to nonengagement; it is an answer reached after considering all options.

Dynamic engagement with technology means that the church is involved in bringing the potential of digital technology to its education, worship, evangelism, or administrative work, or all of these areas. The next, and arguably most critical, step in successful active engagement with technologies for ministry is a very careful, reflective analysis of current needs and areas where technology can be implemented. A well-conceived and broad-based plan should be developed even before the first foray into application is made.

When attempting dynamic engagement, great care must be taken not to unconsciously slip into a *Field of Dreams* mentality. Most of the pitfalls described in the first chapters of this book were based on a kind of "build it and they will come" philosophy. Do the slides with presentation software, build the website, show the film clips during a sermon . . . and they will come. *Field of Dreams* was a wonderful, feel-good movie. My family loved it, and a visit to Dyersville, Iowa, to see the actual field, the farm house, and the ghost players coming out of the corn on the last Sunday of summer months is a joy. But the *Field of Dreams* adage, "build it and they will come," is a terrible foundation for technology planning.[2] (Or any other planning in the church for that matter.)

A Brief Planning Primer

Let's say your church went ahead and bought a Web authoring program like Microsoft's FrontPage or simply downloaded a copy of Netscape Communicator, which comes with a free Web editor.[3] The very first thing you need to do is to put the program away and attend to the planning that will keep your ministry from launching a mistake and possibly closing the door to authentic integration of ministry and technology in your context. The brief guidelines offered here are specifically directed at getting technology planning off the ground. Most people who serve in parish ministry have had little or no training in this area. Maybe you have been fortunate enough to have picked up at least one course in planning. Yet, the introduction of technology into a ministry context is one of those times when planning ability and understanding of your organization is absolutely critical for success. A good book or two in planning should probably go to the top of your reading list ahead of books on creating a good website or using media in worship.[4] Here are six basic steps that will help ensure good beginnings in your hopes for bringing new possibilities to ministry through new technologies.

1. **Develop a total ministry plan**. Just as most congregations have (or wish they had) a children's ministry, youth ministry, educational ministry, and ministry of administration, so they would be well advised to develop a technology ministry. A common mistake congregations make is to view technology in the church as nothing more than asking a few people with computer knowledge to help out. This is both a theological and a practical error. Theologically the church is an organism more than it is an organization. Each member of the body of Christ is gifted to help build up the whole body. Or as Paul put it, "To each is given the manifestation of the Spirit for the common good" (1 Cor. 12:7). When the church is functioning properly as the body of Christ, there are no independent agents. The practical error is that allowing a person or persons to bring technology into the body without connecting it with other ministries of the church will guarantee a disconnect. Development of a total ministry plan requires church leadership to conduct an assessment of the overall ministry of the church and how technology will be integrated.

2. **Develop a total technology plan**. It is important to sketch out a plan for the use of new technologies across the spectrum of the entire church before anything is bought or used. The most common mistake of not planning is that congregations find themselves with lots of expensive, incompatible equipment and software. A Web designer builds a church website on a PC with a software product no one else in the church can use. The Sunday school wants a website, and a couple of high school kids put together a site on a Macintosh. The pastor, meanwhile, begins to use software presentation to illustrate his sermons and tries to use the Sunday school's LCD projector that does not have sufficient lumens to display well in the sanctuary. Over the past few years, a church may have acquired an assortment of five different computers, none of which could talk to each other (meaning they cannot be networked). Creation of a church-wide plan for the use of technology will avoid heartache and costly errors. Christian leaders can learn from the educational world, where information technology has been an especially important issue in the past decade.[5]

3. **Involve all the stakeholders in creating a vision for technology**. If you do not involve the stakeholders, there will be difficulty ahead. Edie Herzog, associate director of Penn State Information Resources said, "Once you have a vision, you have to sell it to users. If people don't buy in, it's constant sorrow."[6] The church does not have "users" (or at least it shouldn't have); instead, we have members. And all the members have a stake in the outcome of any technology plans. Put together a team commissioned by the church's governing body and gather information from the pastoral staff, office personnel, church administrative board, Sunday school teachers, worship leaders, youth group, confirmation class instructors, and anyone else who may have the slightest contact with the church's technology program. When everyone is on board or at least informed about the plans for technology, implementation will go more smoothly.

4. **Plan to address resistance**. No matter how much work is done on a technology plan there will be resistance that needs to be acknowledged. Resistance will be related to three common problems technology induces. Technophobia is simply a fear of technology.

If it's new, different, strange, or mysterious, people will be afraid of it (whatever "it" is). Technology is all these things to many people, especially in the church, which spans the generations.

Technostress is recognition of the fact that technology brings with it a certain amount of additional stress. During one particularly hectic week at work, I was working on my home computer, trying to fix things at midnight, muttering away under my breath, when my wife asked me, "Are you sure you like this work?"

Technobabble is the fault of "techies" who insist on using strange acronyms and highly technical language when talking to "newbies." My program assistant and I were discussing a problem we were having with the compatibility of a video file we wanted to use in a training program. "The file," I was telling her, "is an .mov file, and the PC we want to edit and render the file only reads .avi files. We need to edit on the iMac and use QuickTime Pro to render it out as an .avi. The problem is that the .avi is dark when done on the iMac, so we need to use a filter and render out lighter than we would for a .mov." Our new secretary, who was standing there waiting to give me a message, rolled her eyes, exclaimed, "Oh brother!" and walked out the door. Let me guarantee you that one or two statements like that to your administrative board on the part of your congregation's "super-techie" will buy months of resistance. Your language needs to be "user friendly." Resistance can be overcome by careful explanation, a focus on the good things that can happen with this new medium, patience, and then more patience.

5. **Develop a plan for implementation**. Once a total technology plan is developed, the task will be to create a timeline and begin implementation of your program. It is absolutely essential to focus your technological energy initially on an area that will buy the greatest goodwill and openness for the long-term result you want. Keep in mind that information technology is not wisdom technology. Information is a collection of facts or data. Technology can deliver data easily. Wisdom, on the other hand, is the result of assimilating and assessing information so that it can be successfully applied in the real world. For instance, if the very first film clip you use in worship in a church with a large population of elderly people happens to be the youth group at the Christian

rock concert, that would be using information technology. It might not, however, be very wise. Wisdom might dictate that the very first film clip should be of the church's worship service at the local nursing home. Two final items of caution as you develop a plan for implementation: (a) there is no rush, and (b) there is no rush.

6. **Develop a plan for maintenance**. Who is going to create the website? Who will keep it going a year from now, two years from now, or even five years from now? Where will funds come from for necessary upgrades of hardware and software? How will you evaluate the impact this ministry is having? Quentin Schultze has warned, "We don't have a clue about how to measure effective online evangelism."[7] We can substitute the word ministry for evangelism because the point of measuring effective ministry using technology applies across the board in the church.

The technology ministry team should be involved in every attempt to integrate technology into the life of the congregation. Taking Schultze's word of warning to heart, the team will work on ways to begin the task of evaluating the effectiveness of their work. Three beginning clues to get at the issue of success in integrating ministry and technology are numbers, feedback, and evaluation. Numbers give raw data. How many persons visited the website, came to the multimedia service, or signed up for the online course?[8] Feedback takes the data a step further and provides a measure of receptivity to the activity. It also provides a beginning tool for assessment. Assume 100 people came to a new multimedia service. That would be a positive thing, but if 98 people hated the service, that would not be such a good thing. Feedback will help in evaluating data and moving on to the third clue, which is evaluation. What implications for the ongoing work of ministry and technology emerge from the numbers and feedback?

The emphasis on planning outlined here is important for the introduction of new technologies that represent new opportunities for ministry in the church. The tools necessary for significant ministry in this area are within the reach of more congregations for less cost than ever before.

New Opportunities Using New Tools

I regularly receive phone calls from pastors and church leaders asking if I have a "few moments." After the greetings and pleasantries, the inevitable question surfaces that goes something like this: "We would like to start using technology more, create a website, liven up our worship a bit, and stuff like that. Can you give me a brief rundown on how we might get started?" Requests like this are not unlike asking a lockmaster on the Mississippi River to open up the dam in order to get a cup of water for someone. An adequate answer to the question would result in a virtual flood of information that would leave a muddy mess in its wake. In order to help focus the conversation, I usually respond along these lines: When Christian leaders begin to deal with the overarching issue of how ministry can be enhanced with technology, there are two areas from which everything else will follow. These areas are communication and computers.

Communication comes first. The ancient task of the church is to communicate the Good News of Jesus Christ to all the world and to bring all those who respond to maturity in Christ. Communication is a critical task within the church as well as in the world around us. In order to make use of the remarkable new opportunities digital technologies have made possible, a congregation first has to identify who they want to communicate with. Is the primary concern of the congregation to improve communication within the church for the membership? Is it to reach new people in the community or try new ways of reaching a particular population? Once the issue of *who* is addressed, the next task is to determine *what* it is that needs to be communicated. Do the committee members want more efficient ways to communicate with each other on items of congregational business? Is there a concern to have as much information about church events and church leaders available to a wide group of people on a twenty-four-hour basis? When the who and what of communication have been identified, the issue of computers and peripheral equipment can be addressed.

While the communication task of the church is an ancient one, the computing side of the equation is in its infancy. Computers and computing have brought about confusion for many. The questions can seem terribly complicated. "What kind of computer should we get? How much does an LCD projector cost? How do we get started with Internet ministry? If we buy a computer today, won't it be outdated by tomorrow?" The answer to these questions can be answered when planning has been adequate and questions about communication have been answered. In the next few chapters, we will explore some of the specific ways new technologies can assist in ministry. Before moving on, however, it is essential to set some directions for moving from communication needs to computing capabilities. There are three principles that will guide the process: The planning and implementation of technology should be simple, it should be sufficient, and it should be succinct.

Here's a scenario where the principles might be applied.

It Should Be Simple

A congregation wants to improve communication by making information about programs, members, and service opportunities widely available. The church has also decided to try using visual enhancement through presentation software in worship. Finally, the Christian Education Committee wants at least one computer available for children to use during Sunday school. The pastor has intermediate computing experience, the Christian education director, a volunteer, has a basic knowledge of PowerPoint, and one elder is a programmer for a software company. Two Sunday school teachers are willing to help out, but have no experience with technology. Prior to working on the communication aspects of the church's technology needs and wishes, the group made a commitment to become the ministry of technology team with the pastor as an advisor. The pastor is the only one who has any experience with Web authoring and will teach one of the other team members how to do basic Web editing. The pastor will remain in an advisory role with the team and will not become the church's Web editor.

Application of the first principle to keep the plan simple suggests that the computing and peripheral equipment requirements are for two additional computers. The pastor and secretary both have desktop computers that are approximately three years old. A new desktop will go to the Sunday school in order to meet the minimum specifications for running current software. A laptop computer will be purchased that has adequate capability to process presentation software. The only other requirements to accomplish the identified task are an LCD projector for presentations and Internet access for e-mail. A website in the near future is a likely possibility.

There was discussion of possible future needs for a Sunday school computer lab, replacement of the pastor's and secretary's computers, the possible need for a small network for the church, and additional persons for a worship planning team and a Web ministry team. The first steps recommended by the team to work toward the immediate needs are to secure the Sunday school computer, the laptop computer, and an LCD projector.[9] This plan is not overwhelming to the mind or to the budget.

It Should Be Sufficient

Now the team explores whether its recommendations are sufficient for the task, and a few improvements are made in the plan. The team decides that the laptop can also serve the pastor's needs, and her current desktop computer can be used in the secretary's office by volunteers. The new laptop can also be used in the sanctuary for Sunday services and provide the pastor with mobile computing capabilities. The Sunday school computer and the new laptop will have Windows XP operating systems and the latest versions of Microsoft Office and FrontPage software. The Sunday school computer will be compatible with the laptop and allow for team members to assist with presentation software and Web editing. All team members use the Internet site www.webopedia.com to bring themselves up to speed on any technological terms and acronyms they encounter while doing their homework.[10]

The next steps for the church will be to replace the two older computers in the secretary's office in a second round of technology upgrade. When this is accomplished, the computers will be networked and a higher-end printer integrated into the network. This will allow for sufficient resources in the short term without leading to a dead end in intermediate and longer-term possibilities.

It Should Be Succinct

The team plans to communicate its progress and its plan to the congregation through the newsletter, the announcements during Sunday worship, the printed material in the bulletin, and during a brief explanation when presentation technology is first used in the sanctuary. Guidelines for communication of a technology plan for the congregation are that the articles and announcements be short and to the point, be devoid of technological jargon, deal with immediate, near-term implementation, and focus on the ministry benefit to the congregation. The following article will appear in the church newsletter one month before the first brief media presentation is made in worship:

> On the first Sunday of next month, our Ministry through Media Team will give a short presentation on how our Sunday school children are truly excited about their new lessons on the Gospels. The new computer that you made possible through your generous gifts is currently featuring an exciting new series of Bible stories that the computer is helping to make come alive. Join us for a brief sample and to hear one of the songs they are learning. In coming weeks and months we will be sharing other ways our new ministry will help bring new opportunities to all people of our congregation.

As you can see, a simple, sufficient, and succinct plan and program is the most effective approach. Following these guidelines will not only make for easier planning and implementation but may also curb some resistance. The simpler and more useful a program seems and the easier it is to explain to those not directly involved, the more openness there will be to the program.

Only when such a program is in place and is accepted can the possibilities be truly explored. The next few chapters delve into some of the prospects that the communication and computing solutions can provide for this congregation as well as most other ministries. Armed with healthy hesitation, patience, and persistence, ministry teams have a vast array of choices for enhancing ministry.

New Possibilities for Web Ministry

There is a world market for only five computers.[1]

Tom Watson, Chairman, IBM

There is no reason why anyone would want a computer in their home.[2]

Ken Olson, Chairman and founder, DEC

When it comes to technology and the Internet, predictions of the future are pretty much on par with tarot card readers. "The art of prophecy," Mark Twain declared, "is very difficult, especially with respect to the future."[3] No one could have predicted how expansive the Internet would become. Our language and culture have been radically changed in a mere two decades. The digital revolution ranks with the printing revolution and the industrial revolution. The digital revolution, however, has transformed communication and information exchange in only two decades. Although the roots of computing technology go back to the 1950s,[4] personal computers do not become serious consumer products until the introduction of the first Apple Macintosh and IBM PC in the 1980s. A technology that was unheard of in almost all of recorded history suddenly dominated communication and information exchange. In 1980 there were just under one hundred website hosts. (A website host can support one or more websites.) Then, unnoticed by most of us, that number jumped to one million by 1991. Between 1991 and the present, the Internet has exploded. By the year 2000, the number of hosts for Internet sites topped one billion.[5] It has become almost impossible to count the number of websites that are launched in a year. Over 460 people will become new Internet users in the next ten minutes.[6] In this same ten minutes there will be almost 11,000 new pages of information added to the Internet.[7] In other words, the time has arrived when Internet statistics are all but irrelevant. Suffice it to say that the Internet is humongous.

Flood Control

When Christian leaders and their churches begin to use technology in ministry, they need to be knowledgeable about the digital flood. When personal computers first penetrated the consumer market, memory was measured in kilobytes (abbreviated as K). One byte of information is a unit of storage that is capable of holding one character. A 5¼-inch floppy disk could hold 256K of data. When programs became more complicated and generated more data, hard drives were introduced, and data was measured in megabytes (MB). A 10-megabyte hard drive held just over ten million bytes of information. Ten megabytes sounded like a lot of storage for most home computer use, and few imagined that there would be a need for much more. Mark Twain's quip about predictions proved right once again, however, and hard drives began to be measured in gigabytes (GB). One gigabyte holds just over one thousand megabytes of information. The least expensive home computers now come with 40 gigabytes. These computers, which cost about $750, can store 156,250 times as much data as the old floppy disk that came with my 1986, $3,000-dollar Radio Shack computer. No one imagined a few years ago that a personal computer would ever need a 100-gigabyte hard drive, but I would guess that by the time you read this book, it will be possible to purchase a personal computer with a hard drive or external device that can hold one thousand gigabytes. This calls for a new designation, namely terabyte (a trillion bytes of information). Now imagine millions and millions of computers and servers around the world with the capacity to hold millions of terabytes of information. It is almost as difficult as trying to size up infinity. Remember how God promised Noah the world would never again be destroyed by a flood? That promise has held true, but remember that the reference was to a physical flood made up of H_2O. God did not say anything about other kinds of floods. The world in our time is drowning byte by byte in a flood of digital information.

The relevance of all this for the church or ministry seeking to use the potential of the Internet in its ministry is that the flood of information includes billions of bytes of information that have some bearing on the church. A search for the term "God" on www.google.com yielded 36,700,000 links. A search for "church" produced 25,400,000 hits. This can all be overwhelming. Many who begin the process of exploring the Internet in order to gain assistance for building their own website throw up their hands in frustration. There's simply too much out there. How does one deal with this virtual flood? My recommendation is to ignore the majority of the data available on the World Wide Web. Of the data that remains, only a small fraction will be relevant to your needs.

In order to illustrate in a practical way how technology can be used in the local church, I will follow a hypothetical church as it develops a technology plan. This theoretical church is First Church. As we move through the next few chapters, our hypothetical church will help you to get a handle on how technology can be integrated into local church ministry. First Church is a composite of a number of congregations that have been involved in technology training programs offered at the University of Dubuque Theological Seminary as well as several churches I have consulted with.

First Church Moves Ahead with Internet Ministry

Many churches have discovered that digital technologies once economically out of reach are now eminently affordable. Literally every church can have an effective website. The difficulty they face is the sense of being overwhelmed with information. Where do they begin? What hardware and software are needed? Taking to heart the pitfalls that were spelled out in the first section of this book and following the guidelines in chapter five, the technology team of First Church focuses on what it is that they, as a particular local church, want to communicate, and who they want to communicate with. After careful and prayerful reflection, they reach the conclusion that the primary purpose of a website for the church will be to reach out to the community and seek to draw new people to the life of the church. There is also a secondary purpose to incorporate the needs of the congregation for more effective internal communication and membership services.

During a meeting of the church's governing board, a decision is made to have a special time of "commissioning" during worship for the newly appointed Ministry and Technology Team. The service will be similar to that used for the installation of Sunday school teachers and the church council. This will give visibility to the team's work from its inception and provide an opportunity for the congregation to share a vision for the use of new technologies in the church's ministry.

The team begins its work by conducting random visits to a few church websites to make a list of "dos and don'ts"[8] (mostly don'ts). They also complete a study of the "Web Site Development for Religious Organizations" pages at ReligiousResources.org.[9] This resource is especially helpful for First Church because of its commitment to religious organizations. Two assumptions guide the information provided there: "Money: we assume that religious organizations in general don't have much money to put into the creation and maintenance of their website. People: we assume that much or all of the work of creating and maintaining the organization's website will be done by volunteers in the organization."[10]

After visiting several church websites and studying the recommendations of ReligiousResources.org, the team makes the following basic decisions. They have secured their own domain, firstchurchonline.net for the name of the church's website. This website, with the address www.firstchurchonline.net, is a working website for our hypothetical First Church. You will be able to follow the work of First Church in this chapter as well as in chapter seven by visiting the site. There are several domain name registration services available, but BuyDomains was chosen for its user-friendly administration and value-added services such as e-mail and URL (Web address) forwarding.[11] E-mail forwarding means that any e-mail address that ends with "@firstchurchonline.net" will be forwarded to an existing e-mail address of choice. For example, pastorjohn@firstchurchonline.net, information@firstchurchonline.net, or sundayschool@firstchurchonline.net will all be forwarded to the desired e-mail address. Firstchurchonline.net will be located on the server of the church's current internet service provider (ISP) for the time being. Space for the website is included with the basic fee the church is already paying for its Internet access. This will preclude the necessity of paying for the set up and monthly fee of an actual domain until the size and scope of the website requires it. Anyone who types in www.firstchurch online.net in their browser address window will be directed to the church's home page. The actual address of the website will be something like www.genevaonline.com/~FirstChurch, but one of the value-added services of the domain registrar First Church chose is URL redirection. No matter where the church chooses to host its website, the address www.firstchurchonline.net will always work.[12]

FirstChurchOnline.net will be designed knowing that most people who visit will be accessing the Internet by means of "dial-up" access. This means that graphics and other files that have long load times will not be used. A website committee of three persons will create the Web pages and maintain the site. One of the website committee members will always participate as a member of the ministry and technology team. This will facilitate an integrated approach to the church's overall technology program. Timely updates and fresh content will be high priority items for the website. There will be quarterly evaluations of the church's Internet ministry, which is reported to the church council and congregation. The new Ministry and Technology Team believes that these commitments are essential for an authentic Internet ministry.

These principles for Internet ministry will be in place before a website is authored and launched. A sample website for First Church has been created that follows these principles and incorporates the tools and ideas, which are developed in succeeding chapters. After reading through this chapter, explore the First Church website. The URL is www.firstchurchonline.net. The website of First Church will allow you to follow the steps the church is making as it builds its website.

New Tools for Development

Until recently, some of the more sophisticated tools for websites were available only to groups that had professional Web designers in their midst or the budget to hire professional Web developers. Much of this has changed as high-quality tools for enhancement of a congregation's website have become available. The team at First Church investigates several of these as possibilities for their own use.

Web Logs: Web logs, otherwise known as "blogs," are online magazines that offer a sophisticated way to quickly and easily publish current information or timely articles on the Internet. The Web log is hosted on an outside (third party) server. When someone reads the online magazine, they are actually leaving the church's website and visiting the magazine on another server. Yet, the online magazine is seamlessly integrated with the church website. There is a Web log named First Church E-zine on the sample website. First Church uses the services of Blogger.com[13] for their online magazine, but there are others that can be explored. Blogger offers a free Web log that comes with an advertisement. The advertisement can be removed for a modest annual fee. Fees charged by third party services like Blogger are very much worth the price. Although most Web companies do not allow sexually explicit advertising, a large number of ads are not appropriate for church websites. The ability to easily publish a current, professional-looking online magazine as a part of the church's Internet ministry is a bonus for congregations.

Message Boards: A message board is an interactive tool that can facilitate communication between persons. It is a virtual discussion place. Web logs are edited by one person and used as an online newspaper. A message board is a key ingredient in online learning as the "classroom" or discussion area of a course; it is participatory and collaborative. The only limit to the ways these boards can be used is the creativity of your group. The church might host a prayer group in which the message board is used to share joys and concerns between meetings. The prayer group might also exist as a completely virtual group. Committees might use a message board to conduct business, gather research, and generally facilitate interaction. One advantage of online groups is that members of a group or committee who find themselves pressed for time could use the message board to conduct business. Confirmation classes include both online and in-person gatherings. The First Church sample website includes two examples of how a message board might be used. You can actually visit these parts of the First Church website, post a comment, and read the posts of other readers.

There are two choices when a message board is included as a part of a website. The first is to outsource the message board to an outside source to provide the service, as is done with the online magazine. The second is to purchase the message board software and have it located on your own Web host. Most ISPs will install the software for you. In both cases, the success of the message board is dependent upon having at least one person who will administer the board and ensure that it remains current.

Outsourcing the message board is the less expensive choice, and as is the case with the Web log, a modest fee will provide a message board with good functionality. The board can be customized to integrate seamlessly with the website. The First Church message board is hosted by ezboard.[14] The only disadvantage with outsourcing the message board is that those who participate need to register with the message board owner. It is important for persons who join in the discussion to have very clear instructions about how to register for the service and what this registration does and does not mean. Many people are still wary of providing personal information online. An entry page to the discussion area with clear instructions for moving through the registration process will greet first time visitors.

A second approach is to purchase message board software that is then installed on the same Web server as the church Web. One of the most widely used and highly rated companies that provides message board software is Infopop.[15] This option is slightly more costly and requires that someone on the congregation's Web committee learn to administer the board. The advantage to this approach is that the congregation's message board has the ability to create multiple communities. The Internet ministry committee of First Church decides to do a trial run with an online group powered by ezboard. If and when a determination is made that the message board adds a valuable contribution to Internet ministry, the committee will recommend the purchase of software. The software would provide additional opportunities for community building in the church's ministry. In order to give an example of how the

Infopop message board works, the First Church sample confirmation class uses this system.

Chat Room: There are countless chat rooms in cyberspace where people gather virtually. Many of these are not places you would want your children and teenagers to visit. First Church has its own chat room where teens and their youth leaders can hold virtual meetings. The chat room can be password protected and provide a secure place where they can gather. You can see how this chat room works by visiting www.firstchurchonline.net and then choosing the "Youth Chat" link. To try the chat, have a friend log into the chat room with you. It is available for readers to try at any time. This chat room is also provided by a third party, and for a nominal fee, advertising can be removed.[16]

Our experience with online learning has demonstrated that most adult learners do not care for chat rooms. They are not used to having large numbers of people involved in a single conversation. As participants type their comments, others are doing the same. The resulting text scrolls quickly down the screen. Adults generally find this confusing and chaotic. Young people, on the other hand, seem to be capable of talking to many people at once. They easily follow single conversation threads as they scroll rapidly down the screen woven between other conversations. Chat will be most useful with youth groups, but there are some possibilities for use of chat with adults. This will work best when the chat has only two or three people in the chat room at one time. People who find the price of long distance phone calls prohibitive can log on to the church's chat room and carry on a virtual conversation without cost. Some pastors find a chat room appointment a way to visit with parishioners who are away for extended periods or have moved away, but still retain connections with their home church. An important value of the church chat room is its relative security.

Evangelism: Can evangelism be conducted via the Internet and people brought into a relationship with Christ without that person ever leaving their mouse? "Click here to receive Jesus," one link on an evangelism website says. Does this mean that with one click I am a Christian? This takes the discussion of easy belief to new heights (or depths). Decisions for Christ that do not result in followers of Christ are problematic for a church that has grown increasingly anemic in our culture. Internet evangelism could aggravate an already weakened notion of what it means to be a Christian. How then, shall we think about virtual decisions? Is Internet evangelism possible in any sense?

The Internet Evangelism Coalition has worked to bring about collaboration between groups interested in evangelism in order "to stimulate and accelerate Web evangelism within the worldwide body of Christ, with the partners agreeing to co-labor in the mission."[17] Some coalition members have created evangelism websites that get an A and in some instances even an A+ for technological sophistication. There is, however, not a corresponding grade for growing and maturing disciples. Yet, a visit to these sites is worth the trip to see how the Internet is being used to produce a digital version of an old approach to evangelism.[18] The website NowTryGod.com has been created with the idea that local churches can link to this virtual evangelism brochure from their own websites. At NowTryGod.com, visitors who work their way through the pages are then directed back to the church that provided the link, or they can input their zip codes for a list of nearby churches.

One of the main stumbling blocks of online evangelism is the absence of relationships and community. The context of caring relationships and supportive communities is central to the process whereby the Holy Spirit can bring about the inward turning to Christ that lays the groundwork for transformation. Evangelism in a virtual world created by digital technologies may actually be the antithesis of authentic disciple making.

However, having said all of that, there is a place for evangelism in the church's Internet ministry. A local church website can be one of the ways in which we proclaim good news and seek to enlist followers for Jesus Christ. Relational integrity requires that the Internet ministry of a congregation honestly reflect the character of the people who make up that congregation. If a particular church is in actuality a community of joy-filled, compassionate, caring people who are living out in their corporate life the good news that with God there is hope, joy, and life-changing love, this is news worth sharing with a broken world. The news can be shared by word of mouth, in print media, via the Internet, or by some combination of these methods. First Church will use some of the professional sites as a guide to the eventual design of their own outreach page, but the content of their message will be crafted in light of who they are as a unique congregation.

Evangelism is best accomplished by people who have a relational connection with their community and the people they want to share good news with. Given First Church's desire to have their website reach out to the community where they live, the site is already intentionally evangelistic in the best sense. The church looks for ways it can use the Internet to provide service to the community. First Church evangelism takes the position that it will deliver the good news of God's love by living out concern for the community where they are located. The vast majority of church websites point inward to themselves. First Church wants instead to point to the needs of the community and offer a virtual place where those needs can be addressed. They have asked some tough questions about the role of their website in attending to the needs of the community. "Is there a need for more printed sermons on the Internet?" "Is anyone outside the church crying out for more sermons delivered via streaming media?" "Are unchurched people expressing a desire to see photographs of church buildings or calendars of events for the churches in town?" Answering these questions about community interests and desires can help to foster a more effective online ministry. The website of First Church is aimed primarily at issues of concern to the larger community, whether the visitor is churched or unchurched. We will explore the issue of Internet-based outreach in chapter seven.

The most exciting discovery of the technology team and Internet committee of First Church has nothing to do with technology. They have discovered some new ways people can use their gifts to serve the church. In this process they have also raised some questions about the meaning of church and ministry that can be applied to a wide range of ministries within the church. The worship and education committees, along with others in the church, are beginning to see new ways people can become meaningfully involved in the life of the congregation. A new awareness of the congregation as a community of persons who have been gifted by the Holy Spirit to reach the world around it is emerging. The process of prayer and planning that has gone into the technology ministry is having an impact on other groups in the church.

What Does It Cost?

One of the important considerations for most congregations is the budget requirements of an Internet ministry. The good news is that the website of our hypothetical First Church, which you can visit at www.firstchurchonline.net, can be accomplished with a budget of $709 to $909 for the year. This includes:

- Domain name registration for two years ($36)
- E-zine without ads ($50)
- Message Board without ads (from $60 to $199)
- Chat Room without ads ($75)
- Microsoft FrontPage Web editing software ($169 or use a free program)
- Graphics software[19] ($69 to $99)
- A digital camera ($250 to $400)

If a church can purchase the cheaper camera, or better yet, borrow a member's digital camera and use a team member's graphics and Web editing program to get started, the cost is under $200. No joke! Obviously much more can be spent, but there is no economic reason why any congregation cannot create an attractive Internet presence that can enhance its ministry.

The process First Church is using in its Internet ministry is to move patiently and do less at a higher quality than rushing to publish a website. Anything is not better than nothing, and the early bird does not get the worm when it comes to the publication of church websites. The Internet ministry committee at First Church knows that the initial steps they are taking will build a solid foundation for growing a vital Internet ministry. The work they have done leads very naturally to new possibilities for Christian education and youth ministry. And the great news is that these opportunities are even more of a bargain than the initial website. One of the wonderful things about moving into the field of ministry and technology today is that when you present the ideas in these chapters to your governing body and get the question, "How much is all this going to cost?" you have a terrific answer that governing boards do not hear that often these days. You should get their attention when you tell them,

"Just about $709 for the first year and another $75 for the second year. There is no where else I can think of that we can get more bang for our buck than investing in a well-planned Internet presence."

When the Web ministry is underway and enthusiasm throughout the church is generated, the technology team will turn to other areas as it grows its exciting ministry.

7

Taking Educational and Youth Ministry to the Home

I was astonished beyond all expression. Instead of the ranting, incoherent declarations which I had been told they made on such occasions, I never heard such plain, simple, Scriptural, common sense, yet eloquent views of Christian experience in my life.

James B. Finley
Describing his first experience
in a 19th-century Wesleyan home meeting[1]

First Church Turns to Educational Ministry

The ministry and technology team at First Church is satisfied that the church's Web ministry is doing well and is in good hands with a volunteer group. The next step in their work is to look for ways technology might be applied in the attempt to revitalize the educational mission of the church. They also would like to capitalize on the things that have already been learned in developing the Web ministry. This will keep additional technological learning curves to a minimum.

The team begins by bringing members of the Christian Education Committee together with them for a study of how the Christian church has historically gone about the task of nurturing the faith of its members. They are concerned with addressing the needs of both younger and older members. During their study, they note that small group meetings have always been an effective tool for Christian growth. The small group was the primary means used by the early Wesleyan movement that brought renewal to a large population within the English, and later, the American Church.

A Great New Idea from 1729

How can people in a large and sometimes impersonal institution develop meaningful relationships that nourish personal growth and give support in times of struggle? What happens when a Christian tradition is assimilated into the world to the extent that Christian consciousness has been subsumed by contemporary culture? One significant answer to these questions is found at the very headwaters of the Wesleyan movement most commonly called Methodism. In a short letter John Wesley attached to the first edition of his journal, mention is made of a small group that had begun to gather. He writes, "In November, 1729, at which time I came to reside at Oxford, your son [Mr. Morgan], my brother, myself, and one more agreed to spend three or four evenings in a week together."[2] The group slowly grew at Lincoln College, Oxford and became known as the "Holy Club." Building one another up in small groups where faith and discipline were shared became the key ingredient of a movement that eventually transformed large segments of the church. Frederick A. Norwood in his book, *The Story of American Methodism*, speaks of what it meant to be a member of the group known as Methodists.

> Always central was the idea of close personal fellowship which could be achieved only in a small group. . . . If ever the society or local congregation became too unwieldy, at least in the small class meeting, intimate

community could be maintained. Ideally, no more than twelve would be together under a class leader to meet weekly for spiritual guidance, prayer, Bible study, individual witness, and discipline. Everyone would know, in close personal terms, everyone else.[3]

Class Meetings for Contemporary Congregations

Gathering together in small groups is now and always has been a primary means of building the body of Christ and strengthening its members. Thinking about "church" as a large group is a relatively new phenomenon. Megachurches or absolutely huge churches are a relatively new occurrence on the radar screen of church history. Chances are, when most of us read about the church in our Bibles, we think about the church where we gather on Sunday mornings. In Paul's first letter to the Corinthians, he addresses his letter to "the church of God that is in Corinth." When you hear these words, perhaps you picture a group of people gathered together in your church building. There are stained glass windows, a beautiful altar area, and a narthex where people greet each other warmly as they enter for worship. Maybe the church in Rome brings to mind the large gatherings at St. Patrick's Cathedral in New York, while Paul's more intimate tone in his letter to the church at Philippi may call up a simple Congregational church nestled away in the Green Mountains of Vermont. Intellectually we know this is not the case, but the word church stimulates images we've known since childhood, images that were formed when we were small children wiggling our way through worship services as the adults sang hymns, prayed prayers, and mom did a rib jab on dad as he dozed off during the sermon.

Our ancient brothers and sisters of the earliest church had no such images. The most common expression of the church that was spreading over the known world was small groups of new believers gathering in homes. When church members and denominational executives bemoan the plight of the small church in America today, they are referring to churches that would have been considered large congregations in the apostle Paul's world. True enough, there were large numbers of people in Jerusalem who came to faith under Peter's ministry, but the majority of references to the church in Paul's letters are to small groups of people who met in homes. The church was not the group in the magnificent building sitting on the expensive real estate located at First and Main. It was the church in hiding. In his conclusion to his letter to the church in Rome, Paul asked the people to greet Priscilla and Aquila and to "greet also the church in their house" (Rom. 16:5). In Colossians the writer says, "Give my greetings to the brothers and sisters in Laodicea, and to Nympha and the church in her house" (Col. 4:15).

As the early church was developing, its children were forming vastly different images of church than children of today's churches. They were a part of intimate gatherings of Christian friends where people shared their faith and struggles. They knew that faith in Christ was a costly thing. John Mark, who would have been about a junior or senior in high school, would remember a night when Peter had been put in jail. A small group in his mother Mary's home was praying for Peter's release, but when he was actually set free through divine intervention and showed up at Mary's house, they could not believe the good news. "It must be his angel!" the group exclaims (Acts 12:15 NIV). They thought he had been executed and that his ghost had shown up at the group meeting. Powerful, spiritually formative experiences like this were shaping John Mark's young life as well as the lives of many new believers. There is no possible way an online Bible study or youth discussion group by itself can yield anything close to the formative power of the church under siege in Mary's home or the nourishing influence of a Wesleyan class meeting.

But, if it was possible for technology to provide an assist in the church's attempt to bring people together for spiritual formation in small groups, wouldn't that be worth pursuing? Fortunately, this is not just a possibility. Any congregation can support the building of community in the church through small group interaction with online learning technology. Leaders who are willing to learn the use of simple online learning technology can add significant new opportunities for growth in the church's communal life and educational ministry.

First Church Builds an Online Learning System

The history of the Internet from conception to creation has been written in just over four decades. Until a decade ago, the Internet was essentially limited to military and educational research. Commercialization of the Internet has taken place in just under a decade, with the bulk of this growth coming in the last few years. Most striking of all, however, is that the history of online learning is just now emerging from infancy. There are now literally thousands of e-learning websites available for those who want to take online courses. As is true with owning a website, so it is with online learning: everybody's doing it. But not everybody is doing it well. When a congregation decides to form online Bible study groups or any form of online interaction, it will quickly discover that online groups have an extremely short shelf life unless care is taken to integrate this model of learning with a healthy small group process. Just as a website is not a magic bullet for church growth, so an online learning group will not magically generate mature disciples who are earnestly engaged in the business of following Jesus Christ.

Our hypothetical First Church has made the decision to begin careful experiments with Internet-based learning. The Internet ministry is well under way and is accomplishing the goal of reaching out to the community. The Ministry and Technology Team of First Church is ready to begin using technology in its educational mission. They are cognizant of the fact that meeting virtually cannot replace meeting in person, but virtual meetings beat no meetings hands down.

As First Church ventures into Internet-based learning technologies, they will need to deal with the distinct areas of technology issues and program issues. In terms of the technology issues, they have discovered some good news and some challenging news. The good news is that they already have almost everything they need to begin online classes. The total investment for both the Internet ministry and the addition of an online learning system will still be under $1,000. The technology that was used to create the website, online magazine, and discussion board can be used for online groups without incurring any additional cost. The basic framework of an online learning site is created with the same Web editing program used for the website.

The challenging news has to do with the program issues. The technology for online learning is the easiest part of the equation. Online learning provides an element of convenience for people with busy schedules, but participation in a class and commitment to the group process is more difficult in a virtual environment than it is with a physically gathered group. The convenience is offset by a need for increased commitment and disciplined learners, and the initial pilot groups that I describe a bit later will combine physical and virtual meetings.

In order to maximize the potential for online learning to enhance its educational and youth ministry goals, the Ministry and Technology Team has addressed three areas of concern. They have identified two pilot groups to engage in the process, made provision for the technology that will be used, and set guidelines for participation.

Pilot Groups: As mentioned, the two groups that will use online learning are the confirmation class and an adult Bible study group. The confirmation class was chosen for this venture because the Christian Education Committee had already been discussing ways the confirmation program could be revitalized. The effectiveness of the current program was in question since most confirmands graduated from the church rather than becoming a vital part of its ministry. Time for scheduling classes was increasingly difficult as two-income households struggled to balance school, church, and athletic activities. There was literally no one time slot in the week when all the church's confirmation-age young people could meet at the same time. The confirmation program would have built-in motivation to keep an online program going for the sake of family schedules. Finally, the clientele for the confirmation group is overdue for new approaches that can make use of digital technologies. A question that arises with the use of online learning in the confirmation class is, "What about those who do not have Internet access?" Students without Internet access at home can (a) get access, (b) team up with a student who has access, (c) be paired up with a mentor who has access, or (d) ask the Christian Education Committee to make a computer with Internet access available at the church.

The second group chosen for the pilot project in online learning was an adult Bible study group. The initial group of adults in the program will be made up of people who have consistently expressed a desire to participate in small group Bible study. The group, First Church Online Community, will participate in Bible study, sharing of joys and concerns, a commitment to pray for other members of the group, and reflections on how the group learning and discussion is related to the real world of daily living.

Since these are pilot groups, the effectiveness, as well as the positives and negatives, of the program must be monitored. Two persons from the Christian Education Committee and another from the Ministry and Technology Team have formed a small task group to oversee the pilot groups' experiences. One of the three is a high school student who is active in the church, has a keen interest in technology, authors his own Web page, and happens to have access to a digital camcorder. His background knowledge will be helpful in assessing and utilizing the technology.

Technology: The website has sufficient room to host additional pages for the classes and groups that will be developed. Pages intended for small groups only can be password protected so that only group members can participate. A password page is used by www.firstchurchonline.net for its confirmation class.[4] A discussion board that uses software from Infopop will be added to the site. This will provide a discussion board that is fully under the control of First Church. For the sake of comparison, both the ezboard and the Infopop UBBClassic[5] will be used in the pilot groups. The confirmation class will use the UBBClassic board, and the adult Bible study group will use ezboard. Both of these products were described in chapter six. The confirmation class site will include a chat room powered by Raidersoft.[6] The decision to use a chat room is based in part on the fact that young people are familiar with the medium and are likely to use it as a part of their learning. Besides the discussion board and chat room, the only additional use of technology will be to have all the members and leaders of the confirmation class signed up for instant messaging (IM). Several choices are available for IM, including MSN and AOL.[7] Instant messaging is so widely used by young people that the leaders of the confirmation program want to include it in their design of the program. The youth director of First Church uses IM regularly in contacting the teens.

Guidelines: The members of the task group that is overseeing the pilot project know that a central issue in successful online groups is the interaction of participants and consistent, timely feedback from the class leaders. Online groups are highly dependent upon the self-discipline of the participants. Many online groups begin with great enthusiasm but die a premature death. The tough point comes when the novelty factor wears off and the demands of daily living mitigate against disciplined participation. There has to be some kind of payoff for people who participate. With online students in academic courses, the payoff is a grade. Students in the lay pastor training program offered by the University of Dubuque Theological Seminary must complete their courses in order to be licensed. Online community in this case is formed between people from all over the nation who have no other opportunity to belong to a learning community. The people of the local church, however, are all involved in a voluntary organization in which everything from public worship to attendance at committee meetings to participation in study groups is absolutely voluntary. With confirmation, participation is voluntary for the parents and not so voluntary for most of the students. Nevertheless, the challenge of meaningful participation in online classes with people who are members of the same local church is significant.

Considering all these factors, the online learning team makes a decision that the pilot groups will be hybrid groups. That is to say, they will combine both actual and virtual meetings. The confirmation group, which runs for nine months paralleling the school year, will meet in person once a month. These monthly meetings will involve parents and include an easy evening meal. The adult Bible study group will be an eight week experience with weeks one and eight being in-person meetings in homes, and the intervening six weeks will be virtual meetings. The team is optimistic about the prospects for these groups but very much aware that the price of online convenience is extraordinary commitment on the part of the group members. In order to facilitate this commitment, both groups will begin their experience with a time of covenanting.

Forming the Groups—Covenanting

We should acknowledge that formation of virtual groups in the Christian community, especially in the local church, is an accommodation to the madness of our hectic world. It would be much better if we could gather frequently in groups, but this is not taking place in our world. Consider the following quotation from the Book of Acts and then the translation of the same text from the perspective of a virtual world.

> They devoted themselves to the apostles' teaching and fellowship, to the breaking of bread and the prayers. . . . Day by day, as they spent much time together in the temple, they broke bread at home and ate their food with glad and generous hearts, praising God and having the goodwill

of all the people. And day by day the Lord added to their number those who were being saved. (Acts 2:42, 46–47)

This is a connected group of people. Imagine that this wonderful coming to faith and transformation of lives is all taking place in our time, and we are trying to achieve the same community via the Internet.

> They devoted themselves to the apostles' teaching and fellowship, to the breaking of bread and the prayers. . . . Day by day, they would log on . . . they would dial up or click their "always on" Web access and e-mail their brothers and sisters with glad hearts. They would join in the discussion board as they ate their Big Macs at the keyboard, sharing a prayer with their IMs and praising God with their CCM CDs.

The point is that true community comes only in relationship to the One who created us and connects us with each other. When we use the connecting tools of the digital revolution, we are hoping to build spiritual connections that bring about renewal and new life. It is using the tools of a disconnected world to assist in bringing about transformed lives. The process of gathering in groups that is enabled by technology is intended to emulate Wesley's great idea of 1729, namely, meeting in small, home-based groups for mutual edification, accountability in Christian living, and prayer. When we join with each other in study, prayer, and mutual accountability, we are closer to the ideal of growing together in Christ. In order to facilitate commitment to the online group process, the online learning team of First Church plans to incorporate a time of covenanting in the formation of the trial groups.

A few issues are dealt with in the first meeting for both pilot groups. First of all, there is an introduction of the students and leaders who will be involved. Second, there is an introduction to the technology that will be used. The home where the meeting is held should have Internet access so that instruction and a visit to the website can take place. Then there is some conversation about the purpose and goals of the experience. Finally the issue of community and accountability will be the glue that holds the group together. One of the best ways to accomplish this last step is to make a group covenant that will include a covenant prayer unique to your program. Following is a description of how this covenant session takes place for each of the two pilot groups in First Church.

Constituting and covenanting the confirmation class: The confirmation group leaders, parents, and confirmands gather together for introduction to the online option for confirmation. A meal is served, and the concept of using online technology for the group is explained. Each church will have its own content for the program, but the central issue will be the commitment to the program and to each other as the journey is begun. Care is taken to explain that expectations for the online work are not different than expectations would be for any previous confirmation class. When students do not show up for class, they are likely to be dropped from the class. So also when they do not show up for the online class, it is the equivalent of not attending. A virtual skip is equal to an actual skip. A virtual late assignment is the equivalent of an actual late assignment. If the virtual environment is not working for a student or family, the student will be asked to wait for the next actual confirmation group that gathers. (This is the "payoff" mentioned earlier.)

The group leaders express great optimism for the process and ask the parents to form one circle and the young people another as they recite the following commitment to each other:

> I am counting on you to help me through this new venture to help bring us closer to God's purpose for our lives, and I want you to count on me. I know that I can not achieve the goals of this program without your help and you can not achieve them without mine. In the presence of God and each other, with the help of God and the encouragement of each of you, I commit myself to stay involved until, together, we arrive at the joyful day of confirmation.

Before leaving this initial meeting, parents will pair up and agree to check weekly with each other by phone or by e-mail on progress of the class until the first gathering of parents and students.

Constituting and covenanting the adult class: The adult group has a different set of circumstances than the confirmation class. This is a voluntary gathering of people who have some motivation to grow in their Christian life. The "I have to do this thing" factor will not be present in the way it might be for a confirmation class, but these persons will have to struggle with the need for self-discipline and consistent participation to effectively engage in a virtual group setting. The initial meeting of the group will help in forming the personal connections that can encourage participation. Formation of pairs can be effective in keeping the covenant working. The group uses a similar process to that of the confirmation class as they commit to the online learning experience. In the circle, they affirm:

> I am counting on all of you as we join together to come to maturity in our spiritual journeys. I make myself available to you and promise to be there for you as we commit to this new venture. May God grant us the grace to become all we are created to be as together we embrace this new adventure in following Christ.

The essential function of this process of covenanting to help make the group experience work is to keep the focus on the members of the group and the group process instead of on the technology. Everyone will need to understand that the technological side of the experience is just an aid to what they hope to accomplish. It is not the point. A church's first online groups should be shepherded with utmost care. These initial participants will become the persons who carry the message to other people in the church that the community they experienced was life changing, or they will be an example of how technology is just so much additional busywork that gets in the way.

You can visit the initial two weeks of First Church's pilot groups at www.firstchurchonline.net. Our hypothetical First Church illustrates one way to configure the possibilities of new digital resources for ministry in a church that does not have a large technology budget. Remember, however, that every congregation is unique; application of the technologies used by First Church will need to be individually crafted for particular ministries. The possibilities for using these new technologies are available to every congregation. Keep in mind that small, incremental steps are best. In the field of ministry and technology, later is better than sooner if planning and preparation are not complete. Rushing the process will ensure a quick exit from what might have been an excellent partnership in the church's Christian educational ministry.

A final area of new possibilities in ministry using new technologies is the use of images and imagination in worship and learning. This offers us not only a new way to use images but some new insight into exploring God's truth through images.

8

The Sphinx's Smile

That night my imagination was, in a certain sense, baptized;
the rest of me, not unnaturally, took longer.[1]

C. S. Lewis

Images as Messages

It is the Sunday after Christmas and the pastor of First Church has chosen the Gospel lectionary text, Matthew 2:13–23. Through focusing upon the story of the flight into Egypt, the pastor wishes to make the basic point that Christmas is far more than good feelings and nostalgic warmth. Instead, the birth of Jesus stirs up the worldly powers (King Herod, for instance) that are enraged by the potential displacement of their authority by the little baby. The pastor knows that this is not an easy message to comprehend because of the Christmas season's identification with peace and good cheer. Therefore, she has chosen to take advantage of the new technological capacity of her congregation—an LCD projector.

After reading the text and introducing the basic theme, the pastor states, "Probably most of us imagine Christmas like this . . ." and then

111

she cues the first picture in the LCD projector. It is Frederico Fiori Barocci's *Rest on the Flight into Egypt*.[2] "Here is a joyful picture," the pastor continues. "Everybody seems to be having a great time. Joseph and Jesus are playing together. Mary is content. Even the donkey appears to be smiling. The holy family seems absolutely delighted in their new refugee status!" Many in the congregation laugh, understanding the overstatement.

The pastor continues, saying that although this is the common impression of the holiday, in reality, the flight into Egypt was very different. The dark powers of the world were still very present and active as this family ran for their lives. The pastor then cues the second picture. Once again, it is a depiction of the same theme, but this time the picture is Adam Elsheimer's *The Flight into Egypt*.[3] This clip stresses the very real struggles of the holy family. Then she points to the hope breaking into the picture. As dark as Elsheimer's night is, there is still light—the light of the stars and full moon, the light of a campfire, and most beautiful of all, a strange light that hauntingly illuminates Mary, Joseph, and Jesus. She reminds the congregation, "Here is the true power of Christmas—the shadows of this broken world like King Herod darken and threaten, but they cannot overwhelm the newborn King." The contrast of the two pictures seems to be working. The people are engaged and following the sermon.

The third and final point to the sermon is that Christmas is a season of true hope. The pastor announces, "In the end, the powers of this world will serve the purposes of God. They may have their own plans—they may have their own desires, but the powers of this world will all eventually acknowledge the authority of this child." Here, the pastor cues the third image. Once again, it is another illustration of the same theme, but this is an interesting variation on the subject. Luc Olivier Merson's *Rest on the Flight into Egypt*[4] takes seriously the Egyptian locale. The most striking aspect of the painting is that Mary and Jesus are resting in the arms of a sphinx!

The pastor points to the image and declares, "Look, brothers and sisters—see how even the pagan deities—the false gods of this world must serve the baby Jesus. They have their own power, they have their own authority, but they are still under the authority of the true God who has loved this world enough to send his Son. And perhaps even here the powers of this world have discovered their own vocation, for is that not a smile on the sphinx's face? This is the heart of our hope. Christmas has not completely stopped the forces of darkness in our world. King Herod still rages. But the true hope and promise of Christ's authority is that all these powers will eventually serve the good purposes of God." As they leave church that Sunday, a number of parishioners comment on the power of the sermon. One observes, "Pastor, I had never seen that in the text. I'm certainly glad that we invested in this new technology. I don't think that I'll ever think about Christmas in exactly the same way."

Now imagine a second church. It is still the Sunday after Christmas. At Second Church, the congregation has also invested in a technology upgrade. The pastor of Second Church wants to preach on the same text and also illustrate the true power of Christmas. He is preaching a good sermon; the people are following the several points closely. In the conclusion, the pastor desires to illustrate that joy can still be discovered even though darkness is present. He cues the LCD and a video clip from the cartoon version of *How the Grinch Stole Christmas*⁵ begins to play. It is the scene wherein the Whos of Whoville react to the realization that their Christmas has disappeared overnight. "Look, look!" says the pastor. "All the trappings of Christmas are gone. But the Whos do not despair. Instead, they sing. The truth of Christmas cannot be stolen. Darkness may be present even at Christmas. But it cannot overwhelm the truth of what God has done in Christ."

The people of Second Church congratulate the pastor on another fine sermon. They have particularly enjoyed the video clip and many more are now convinced that the technological upgrade was well worth the cost. But the pastor is somewhat taken aback as one parishioner says to him as he exits, "Thanks, pastor. That video sure reminded me of a lot of my happy Christmases as a child. Wouldn't it be great if Christmas could be as meaningful for us as it is for kids?"

Technology Awakens the Imagination

Unfortunately many pastors and/or congregations probably do not have a theory of the theological role of technology in worship. For many, as with the parishioner from the previous story, the film clips or projected images are simply more sophisticated versions of the traditional opening joke of the sermon. They are a means of arresting the attention of the listener (and now viewer) sitting in the pew. Having gained the viewer's attention, others are now using PowerPoint presentations, such as projected outlines, in order to hold the interest of the congregants. Technology functions as a more stylish way of place-marking. The worshipers can now know at all times approximately how much longer the sermon will last because they are able to follow an outline projected on a screen. Information is revealed before one's very eyes as words appear in the outline's blanks. This use of technology could cause one to conclude that the faith is not so much a mystery to be explored as it is a puzzle to be solved.

It seems then to be the case that the primary uses of the new technology are familiar ones. Projected images are used to entertain and/or to impart information. They are effective tools for enlivening the Sunday morning or Saturday night experience. The purpose of this chapter is not to argue for or against the place of either entertainment or information passing during worship. Instead, it is to explore the other effects technology has, especially the possibilities projected images, be they moving or still, hold for engaging the viewer's imagination.

One of the best opportunities digital technology can offer to the worship experience is a new ease in the creation of visual presentations. Such visual presentations can readily engage the viewer's imagination. In the next several years, such presentations will cause theologians and other church leaders to give more thought to the role of the imagination in both evangelism and discipleship. Historically, much time has been spent targeting reason (as in apologetics) and the emotions in sermons and other presentations of the Christian message. Relatively little attention has been paid to the imagination.

Yet it may well be the human faculty of the imagination that plays the key role in fostering one's relationship with God. The imagination has been described as "amphibious."[6] Living in both the worlds of reason and fantasy, the imagination allows us to make the transition between what is and what could be. Offering a vision of existence other than the one we presently know, the imagination allows one to "step out in faith." The imagination transforms nonexistence into possibility. But the very gap-spanning nature of the imagination demands a certain degree of raw material with which to work.

To return to the opening illustration, we discovered two churches, two sermons on the same text, two attempts at using the new technology.

Both pastors engaged the imaginations of at least some of the worshipers. Yet one seems to have communicated the basic message much more clearly than the other. The mixed message of the second sermon was both less and more than what the pastor had in mind.

The two sermons illustrate both the promise and the pitfalls of using technology for the purpose of engaging the congregants' imaginations. The images utilized in First Church seemed to capture the imaginations of some of the congregation. They opened up a new means for understanding the message of the text. In particular, the images stimulated a new way of thinking about one of the most familiar stories of Christianity. At least one reason for the success may be attributed to the lack of familiarity that most of the congregants had with the images. Their lack of earlier associations with the images allowed the preacher greater freedom in channeling the imagination. Thus the preacher's intended message closely coincided with what was perceived by some of the congregants.

On the other hand, the mixed results at Second Church show well the necessity of better understanding the role of imagination in worship. That preacher also engaged the imaginations of some of his congregants. But, by choosing a familiar set of images (from *How the Grinch Stole Christmas*) the preacher elicited more than what he had intended. The imagination of at least one congregant went to work and caused a nostalgic immersion.

A Powerful New Force

Using images in worship can aid in the delivery of a message. In addition to the sense of sound, it engages another sense, the sense of sight, which then enables the viewer to make different connections with the material. This is not the first technological advance to capitalize on a new sensory organ previously untapped. As mentioned in chapter two, LCD projectors in worship may very well begin to function as did the printing press in the sixteenth-century Protestant Reformation. Peter Matheson has recently written:

> The reforming process was not fundamentally about ideas in the mind or structures in church and state but indicated much more elemental

changes in spiritual direction. These are signposted by the creative meta-phors of the preachers and teachers, the images in literature and art, the rhythms and melodies of the popular ballads and chorales which sang the Reformation into people's souls.[7]

The new printing presses not only produced the words of Scripture but also vivid pictures to illustrate the Bible. Matheson's basic argu-ment is that people's lives were changed not only by biblical doctrines but also by renewed biblical metaphors. One might further argue that the acceptance of the doctrine was dependent upon first changing the metaphor or mental picture. This, then, created a new world (a new place to stand) in which the doctrine could be appropriated. But without a change in the images, there could have been no appropriation of the "new" ideas of the Reformation.

It is most certainly premature to state whether or not the church stands on the brink of a new reformation ushered in by the new tech-nology. Instead, I seek only to caution preachers and worship leaders in their use of the new technology. Images can and do engage the imagination. And the imagination plays a powerful role in enabling the congregant's ability to grasp the "strange new world within the Bible."[8] Worship leaders and preachers should be much more cautious and intentional in their utilization of images in worship. They are not neutral tools, but instead, they have the power to either enable or disable the perception of the message. Imaginations will be engaged, but to what end?

It is no accident that many Protestants have failed to understand the power of images and metaphors in worship. Citing the work of David Tracy, Andrew Greeley has spoken of "the two different ways of approaching the divine reality that arose out of the Reformation."[9] He notes that "the Catholic imagination loves metaphors; Catholicism is a verdant rainforest of metaphors. The Protestant imagination distrusts metaphors; it tends to be a desert of metaphors. Catholicism stresses the 'like' of any comparison (human passion is like divine passion), while Protestantism, when it is willing to use metaphors (and it must if it is to talk about God at all) stresses the unlike."[10]

The Protestant reticence toward metaphors may help explain the lack of reflection about the role of technology in worship. Protestants are rather inexperienced in using pictures. Because they have been far quicker to say how an image fails than how it succeeds in evoking God's saving work, Protestants have tended to be rather hesitant about utilizing images.

Furthermore, is not the spoken sermon the centerpiece of traditional Protestant worship? Thus, Protestantism has been "ear-focused." As with metaphors, many Protestants have been very suspicious of "eye-focused" images, if not completely hostile toward them. Therefore, it is no surprise that Protestants would tend to understand images as things to utilize for the purposes of entertainment and information. The traditional Protestant focus breeds an underestimation of the power of images.

Yet in spite of this lack of reflection (and open hostility) concerning images, Protestants, through the new technology, are using them. In part, this may signal an unreflective understanding that people yearn for far more than entertainment and information in worship. Perhaps it marks a growing realization that the more information dominates our time, the less able we are to think in any other way. Therefore, worship must be more than figuring out the right answers to the problems of living. It is not more information that people need, but instead an imaginative leap—a new way of seeing and thinking. Jesus' way of prompting this leap involved the telling of short, pithy stories: parables. They were not primarily instructional, but rather revelatory. Their primary purpose was not to "inform" but to "form."

People are seeking far more than humor and "filling in the blanks." As they have always done, images and their linked metaphors make possible the imaginative leap necessary for envisioning the kingdom that dawns in the life and message of Jesus Christ. Many worship leaders are beginning to comprehend this and are becoming increasingly excited about the possibilities which the new technology offers.

Taming the Wild Imagination

Again, it must be remembered that images are not easily domesticated, instead they frequently surpass or fall short of the preacher's intended purposes. This occurs for at least two reasons.

First, as we have noted, familiar images will evoke many things. A picture really is "worth a thousand words." The preacher or worship leader has no way of completely controlling where any given image will take the viewer. As stated earlier, the unfamiliar may often work better because of the limited associations the viewer can make. But this is no guarantee of success. If the film clip, although never seen before, features a familiar actor, it may very well cause the viewer to think of the actor's other roles. Showing the unfamiliar clip of John Wayne as the centurion at the cross in *The Greatest Story Ever Told* may prove the point of the sermon. On the other hand, some may find it impossible to hear "the Duke" attest to Jesus being God's Son without still thinking of shoot-outs and cattle drives.

Another reason for the failure of images in worship stems from the increase in American culture of biblical illiteracy. People no longer have a familiarity with the basics of the Christian story. Many images may be completely lost on the folks occupying the pews. Being overly subtle may be very dangerous. Images can help initiate people into God's kingdom, but they are certainly not enough. In C. S. Lewis's terms, imaginations must be baptized.[11] However, it is very important to remember that baptism is at the beginning of the Christian life. The imagination needs reasonable instruction even as reasonable instruction needs the imagination. Images continue to need explanations as much as explanations continue to need images.

Therefore, it must never be forgotten that images can illustrate beautifully, but they can also confuse. They can both strengthen and undermine the preacher's words. The preacher must be careful in his or her use of the new technology in worship for it does indeed have a life of its own. The imaginations of congregants will certainly be engaged through both the visual and the auditory stimuli. Yet, the question remains: Will their imaginations lead them to the place that the preacher intended?

Still, in conclusion, return to the third of the images used at First Church, Merson's *Rest on the Flight into Egypt.* The smiling sphinx illustrates my purpose.[12] The sphinx represents a pagan power brought into the saving activity of God. It smiles in its delight to be of service to the little King. Like the sphinx, the new technology can certainly be brought into the service of God. It can play a dramatic role in touching the imaginations of the people in the pews. It can indeed open to them the metaphors necessary to perceive God's saving activity. It can help span that gap between the nonexistent and the possible. It can "form" instead of merely "inform," so long as the worship leader always asks,

"What will the viewer make of this image? Will this image help the viewer move across the gap between the 'what is' and 'what could be'? What is the worshipper being formed into?"

Like the sphinx, the people may be smiling, but do we really understand why?

Part 3

Study
the Practice

Ministry and Technology— It's All About Ministry

> . . . we need to . . . do what Paul was doing, bringing the
> new reality of Christ's Lordship into an engagement with the
> context in which our hearers live, in order to point the way to
> new life in Christ.[1]
>
> Nancy Lammers Gross

First Things First

For just over three years, Dubuque Seminary has been training pastors in the integration of new technologies in ministry.[2] We are very clear about priorities. Ministry comes first. Technology comes next. Technology training is widely available in junior colleges, universities, and independent computer training centers. Multimedia companies that specialize in selling to the church market offer workshops in using technology in the church.[3] While instruction in using digital media in worship and other forms of ministry is becoming increasingly available, the focus is usually on the technology and "how to do it," rather than on the ministry it is intended to build. Look carefully at these three forms of the phrase Ministry and Technology:

MINISTRY and TECHNOLOGY
~~MINISTRY~~ and TECHNOLOGY
MINISTRY and ~~TECHNOLOGY~~

If you eliminate ministry, all you have left is technology. If you eliminate technology, you still have ministry. One of our students said, "I have taken computer and other technology courses in the past, but until now I have not had any guidance in how to put this all together in ministry."

When congregations and religious judicatories begin to explore the possibility of training existing staff or hiring new staff to work in the area of ministry and technology, it is important to spell out the skill set that will be necessary. The following vision statement for our training program may help you focus the skills and commitments that will be essential for balanced, ministry-centered staff in your own context.

> The vision behind this program is to train persons who are equipped to use new technologies in the service of the church. At the same time our intent is that these persons have competence in theological-spiritual reflection in the application of technology in the ministry of the church. The "Minister of Technology" is a person who is competent in technology, grounded in the Christian faith, and committed to the Great Commission by all available means.

All students are required to complete a capstone project that will make a significant contribution to the life of the church or judicatory they serve. I want to explore a few of these projects with you that can serve as models of new avenues for ministry in the wider church. The particular examples are chosen for the wide range of application of digital technologies in ministry. Whether it is application of new approaches to established ministries or new ministries altogether, these projects are opening up possibilities for ministry and involving people in service.

A New Look at Confirmation

One project was aimed at enhancing the confirmation program of a local church by involving the students in the use of technological tools in a variety of ways. Confirmation students had the opportunity to interact with each other and with the wider church through a website published on the church's Web space. The congregation would be kept aware of the progress and activities of the class through a site that would be authored and updated by the teens. Integration of a chat room with the site gave the class a way to be in touch between class meetings. A message board for parents is an option in which a support group dealing with topics relating to teens provides community for parents of the confirmation students.

Confirmands were paired with adult mentors with a view to having the young people become more active within the church. Each team developed presentations using images to illustrate the Psalm of the day. A second assignment was for students and mentors to visit shut-ins in a nursing home and bring video of the visit, which was used in prayer time during worship. A final segment of the new confirmation class was an online learning component in which students used online resources to research topics in the confirmation curriculum. The topics were then discussed on a message board. Through this class, the students had an opportunity to be involved in the use of media in worship, online learning, and reaching out through visitation and prayer. Technology provided a way for the wider church to stay in touch with its young people, who were preparing for their public confession of faith. The nursing home visits provided a fully intergenerational opportunity that had an impact on the whole congregation.

Through application of new technologies in an established ministry, involvement of new people in the traditional confirmation class, and reaching out to the nursing home residents, this program has created a broad-based openness to the use of technology in ministry.

Reaching Out to the Wider Church

One pastor chose the wider church for the focus of his project. Just over eighty churches, many of them of small and medium size, belong to a presbytery that has a desire to determine how new technologies can help them assist local churches. Aiding congregations in their mission and improving communication between all parties is at the top of the priority list.

The initial task is to complete a comprehensive evaluation of the ways technology is currently being used in congregations and to help local churches evaluate current needs. There will also be sessions for envisioning possible future uses of technology. When the results are gathered, they will be shared through the Internet as well as through multimedia presentations. These presentations will be taken to local churches and placed on CDs for distribution to congregations. The completion of this process will assist the presbytery in determining whether a staff person skilled in the use of technology and rooted in parish ministry is necessary to maximize the new opportunities that are available.

The project was crafted in light of the need for a patient, theologically informed, spiritually balanced application of ministry principles in the assessment of technological need and opportunities. A critical principle in this project is that the judicatory will begin with its constituents in making an assessment of the need for technology. Many judicatories have made the "upside down" mistake in which the great ideas for using new technology come from the top down. This usually guarantees a score of zero in relevancy to the actual needs of those who are supposed to use the technology. In this project, the student wrote, "This information will help the presbytery discover whether or not there is a need for a staff person that is specialized in technology, as it pertains to its churches."[4] This is a refreshing change in a world where decisions about what local churches need are made by persons who are not *in* the local church. This principle is built into our instructional schema whereby all constituencies are consulted and involved in the formulation of plans and the implementation of technologies.

A Passion for Prayer

One of the projects emerged from a long process of study, reflection, and work by a local church pastor. This pastor is a member of a shrinking minority group. He has been pastor of the same local church for over twenty-five years.[5] During these years, he has developed a strong commitment to the idea that a personal spiritual life is dependent upon a strong prayer and devotional life. His project is based on an eighteen-year study of the Psalms. The plan was to develop a thirty-day personal devotional study based on the Psalms that could be shared with a wide audience through the Internet, on CD, or in printed form. This work is another example of how new digital resources can be used in an area of ministry that is historic. This new approach to prayer and Bible study is a refreshing application of new tools. It is not aimed at the "new and flashy," but at widening accessibility in historic disciplines.

The heart of the project is a website with a thirty-day study of the Psalms. It includes artwork, the text of the Psalm, and questions for personal reflection. The beauty of this project is that families, church members, and wider church groups can journey through this thirty-day devotional period regardless of time or location. A family with a mother or father who travels for work can "log on" and join the family in study. The study can be facilitated with a chat room and message board so that persons may stay connected regardless of time and geographic constraints. This project points to exciting and creative new ways technology can be used to nourish Christian living.

Opening Doors through Online Study

One of the students in the Dubuque program is a senior pastor in a multiple-staff church. He has led the congregation in using new technologies for building a Web ministry, expanding opportunities in worship, and making use of online learning. The particular ministry he was most excited about was the online class on discipleship he had worked with. He wrote about the group that agreed to work with him by participating in the church's first online class:

> Let me tell you about my online discussion experience! It has been one of the most incredible discussion moments in my time as pastor here in Lawrence. I have witnessed discussions in a different way than any Sunday morning discussion. We had 35 people say that they would like to participate, but it has been more like an average of 20. I have tried to respond to every person's comments and that has been more fun than a burden.

Yesterday I called one person who has been participating each week. She has made some major statements of feeling lost in the crowd at this church. This week she said that she has now decided that the problem is not that people are not seeking her out but that she is holding back from reaching out to others! I called her yesterday and said that I could not put a face with her name and asked if she would please introduce herself the next time she was in worship. She was thrilled that I called and promised me she would do that.

It's interesting how the discussion changes from week to week. When people started they seemed reserved, but not now. It is almost as if a new class has been formed . . . and now they do not want it to end. They are now asking if we can continue this type of discussion.[6]

During the online study, two participants in the group had to relocate. The online class experience became a lifeline for them as they left their church and friends. The connection that was maintained through the online experience created a strong bond between people who could no longer gather in a physical way. This model holds promise for congregations where members move away from the community but retain strong ties with the church.

These projects represent just a few of the possibilities that continue to grow as pastors use new tools for ministry in imaginative ways. A repetitive theme throughout this book and throughout the ministries of people who have come for training is that these new tools find their most productive and ministry-enhancing use in the local church. When local church pastors, leaders, and members join together in making use of new technologies, the ideas and new applications continue to amaze those of us who teach.

Ministry and Technology—Whose Ministry?

I have emphasized throughout this book that success in ministry using technology depends upon mutuality in ministry. Students in our program are committed to the precept that ministry has been given to all of God's people. The pastor is the "guide on the side" rather than the "sage on the stage." Much has been written about lay ministry over the years in which pastors are described as enablers, coaches, equippers, and other terms that point to a model of ministry as ancient as

Scripture. The title of Melvin J. Steinbron's book, *Can the Pastor Do It Alone?*, asks the very question that needs to be asked at the outset of every attempt to use technology in the church.[7] On the surface, the question can be answered in the affirmative. Yes, it is possible for the pastor to do it alone, but it is not prudent for the pastor to do it alone. The easiest thing for students to do in the near term is to return to the parish, begin using media in worship, put together a presentation with graphics and film clips, set up the computer and LCD projector, and dazzle the congregation. The problem is that this would be the kiss of death for lay ministry in the long term. Solo ministry is precisely the thing we are working against. It would be a great idea if we could indelibly print a sign on the consciousness of every clergyperson who gets excited about ministry and technology: *Do not do this work alone!* As we share the good news of the potential for ministry in a digital age, our key question is, "Whose ministry is this?" Our program is not called "The Pastor and Technology" or "Clergy and Technology" for a reason.

While the issue of lay ministry is not limited to the field of "Ministry and Technology," successful implementation of new technologies in ministry does depend on significant lay involvement in ministry. Possibilities for the use of new technological capabilities are so great and the work to properly use these new opportunities is so enormous that the "lone ranger" approach to ministry is the single greatest threat to success. On the other hand, a "lone rangerism" of clergy is so deeply ingrained in the contemporary church that a change in style does not come easily. When our students complete their first residency we enjoin them to "form a ministry team for this work as your very first assignment when you get home." This injunction goes against the grain for a large number of pastors and their congregations. The disconnect between what many churches profess about lay ministry and what they practice is scandalous. How many church signs and church bulletins proclaim something along the line of "Pastor: John Doe, Ministers: All the Members." In most instances, this affirmation of lay ministry is not backed up by the practice of lay ministry. The need for significant involvement of laypersons in the implementation of the new technologies in ministry may well lead the way in lifting up the importance of lay ministry in the whole church.

Costly Pearls

Speaking of the kingdom of heaven, Jesus said, "the kingdom of heaven is like a merchant in search of fine pearls; on finding one pearl of great value, he went and sold all that he had and bought it" (Matt. 13:45–46). Everything of real value in advancing the kingdom of God is costly. Any approach to ministry that promises quick or easy steps to revitalization of the church and large increases in membership are suspect. Kingdom work is hard work, but it is rewarding work. Authentic integration of ministry and technology is dependent upon the commitment of all parties. Do not underestimate the deep commitment that is necessary in this work.

When you engage the work of integrating technology into ministry, there will be times when you feel what one of our students expressed in an e-mail note. This takes us back to some of the pitfalls we discussed in part 1 of this book—but it does bear repeating.

> In a word I can summarize the last few months—*Frustration*. I've been doing techie stuff for twenty years now, and the constants I've experienced directly because of technology are *stress, frustration*, and a nagging sense of urgency. Lately our family has been trying to identify those elements that can make our lives simpler since simplicity is a spiritual discipline. I am convinced that simplicity is much closer to the heart if you factor out all the technological sludge. Get rid of the computers, the remotes, the stereos, the mp3s. Get rid of all of it, and life slows down. Technology serves to speed life up and with that increase in speed comes an impatience that is a true evil, complete with demonic obsessions. If we are about spiritual fitness and wholeness then we need to rethink how to do technology so that technology doesn't do us. The Amish lifestyle sounds pretty good right now.[5]

Learning *"how to do technology so that technology doesn't do us"* is excellent advice indeed. Once the particular issues that generated this student's stress were dealt with and spiritual balance returned, he returned to his work and technology project. The lesson behind this should be taken to heart. Without a disciplined spiritual life and solid grounding in theological disciplines, technology is no friend of ministry.

Frustration is a part of the mix, yet the bottom line for the field of ministry and technology is that beyond the frustration, there is a world of opportunity that can make a significant and positive difference in ministry. Another student acknowledges frustration, but points to the opportunities.

> While I have had my share of frustrations — over all my experience has been fun, exciting, eye opening, rewarding, and over all fantastic! I was surprised at my older age congregation's acceptance of the use of power point in worship. We repeated the program I designed last year for Veteran's Day and we had members of the congregation in tears — followed by many excellent comments. Also when we used it on Christmas Eve last year it was openly accepted and enjoyed even by those who want a "traditional" service. We will use power point again for Christmas Eve this year. I have been stretched and challenged — but have loved every minute of it.[9]

As I hear from pastors and Christian leaders who are charting new ground with innovative ways of using digital media in ministry, I am amazed and grateful. Stories of the costly but precious pearls of meaningful ministry continue to come to us.

In one confirmation service that I was privileged to witness, a brief video presentation of the young and growing years of each confirmand was projected as background music from youth choirs they had sung in during their years of growing up in the church. The children's voices quietly filled the sanctuary during a brief presentation for each young person as they came forward to kneel for the prayer of confirmation. I did not even know these young people personally and I was misty-eyed. The power of images, music, and the great traditions of the church came together in a wonderful blend of old and new. This approach to the use of image and music holds tremendous potential for special services like All Saints Sunday, weddings, and even funerals. Undoubtedly, Christian leaders who are now becoming equipped to use these new tools in ministry will write the last chapters of how ministry flourished in a disconnected world.

One of the most productive ways to get at the heart of how ministry and technology can be integrated successfully is to listen to the stories of those who have made the journey you are hoping to take. I want to take you to a short case study of a congregation that has managed to live out the premise that it is "all about ministry." Union-

Congregational Church in Waupun, Wisconsin, has been growing its ministry-in-media enhanced worship for almost five years. Their story is especially instructive for the vast majority of us who live and minister in the small- and medium-size congregations where most Americans live.

10

Worship that Connects

We are more impressed by a church of 4,000 people who don't have a clue about God's character and His expectations, than by a church of 100 deeply committed saints who are serving humankind in quiet, but significant ways.[1]

Sally Morgenthaler

Good Things—Small Packages

Hundreds of ducks are honking on final approach to Horicon Marsh as I wind my way into Waupun, Wisconsin. It is a clear, crisp, mid-November morning and the drive along Highway 151 is easy and traffic free. Waupun is just about an hour from Madison, Wisconsin, to the southwest and Milwaukee to the east. In some ways, this is an unlikely journey for a field study in the use of technology in worship. I am on my way to spend a morning with a medium-size congregation in a small Midwestern town that has spent the last five years patiently building a successful multimedia worship service. A number of years ago, attendance at the church had reached a plateau of two hundred worshipers. Today, the multimedia worship service alone runs about that same number.

But why not head south the short distance to Chicago, Illinois? Chicago has hundreds of large churches, many of which have expensive equipment, sophisticated media-enhanced Sunday morning experiences, and expert staff that oversee a professional production process. Why not visit a church where there is more—more technology, more people, more staff, and more professionally produced media? There are two main reasons.

First of all, I have visited a number of large congregations where media is used with near perfection and attendees are treated to polished, professional presentations. When these services are over, people say things like "Wow!" as they might after seeing their first *Star Wars* movie on the big screen. I've said "Wow," a couple of times myself. There are always comments along the line of "Impressive, huh?" "That was a great show!" "I was blown away!"[2] There is no question that these experiences have an impact on those who participate in them. The key issue is whether the experience constitutes authentic worship that connects the worshiper with God and the community of faith or whether the participants are more like spectators who have been entertained. Is the impact of the presentations a spiritual one?

This is not a debate about whether multimedia itself encourages passivity in the worship setting. In his book, *Silver Screen, Sacred Story*, Michael Bausch, in a section entitled "Just Sitting There," argues correctly that passivity in worship is as much a possibility in a word-oriented worship as it is in multimedia worship.[3] Using multimedia in worship in a way that connects people to God and to each other and overcomes the disconnective pressures of contemporary living begins long before the actual worship experience.

Union-Congregational Church in Waupun integrates multimedia in worship in a way that connects worshipers with God and each other. The secret is in how they plan, produce, and practice the media ministry. It is a difference between participatory ministry and professional production. The former flows naturally from within the life of the congregation, while the latter is produced by a few for the consumption of many.

The second reason for choosing Waupun (other than the joy of a leisurely drive in the country instead of the freeway frenzy of Chicago) has to do with what can happen in smaller congregations when ministry and technology are properly integrated. Although the large and super-large churches get most of the publicity and commercial enterprises that target the church technology market, the potential of the small-to-medium-size congregation to reach our culture is mind-boggling. A megachurch may reach thousands of people on a weekend and see thousands join their ministry in a year. Megachurches, including new media-driven megachurches, draw a lot of attention, sponsor many conferences, and inspire people to be like them. In a culture where bigger is better and church parking lot traffic jams mean success, it is easy to ignore smaller sources of inspiration. Yet, large congregations make up just ten percent of the 300,000 churches in America.[4] This leaves 270,000 smaller congregations deployed all over the country—most of whom are seeking ways to revitalize their ministry.[5] The journey of Union-Congregational Church and its people in multimedia worship is a much more likely source of inspiration for the majority of us. Union-Congregational Church has reached close to two hundred new people in the past five years. The math alone affirms that the experience in Waupun has more potential to bring new life to the church than do all the megachurches. It is more than math that makes the difference, however. It is the method by which the multimedia ministry has grown as an effort of a whole community of faith. This congregation is led by a pastor who believes ministry is the privilege and the responsibility of the whole people of God.

It's Not About Technology—Beginnings

Interest in the multimedia worship service at Union-Congregational Church has grown as word of its growing ministry has spread. Yet, the beginning of the ministry was not about technology at all. It began with a pastor who exhibited two essential characteristics. First of all, he was committed to a collegial style of leadership and had the patience to allow all the good ideas to come from the people of the church. He stimulated people to ask the question, "How can we reach out to the unchurched people of our community?" Second, he was a musician, literate in visual arts, and knowledgeable about the ways television and film have had an impact on our culture.

With patience, prayer, and persistence, a team began to plan a short series of services where media, including video clips displayed on a television set, would illustrate the theme of the biblical message chosen for the day. In the beginning, a handful of people came. But those who did come were truly engaged with the message. One of the leaders of the church's multimedia worship planning team said, "We have always worked to keep the message our priority, it was never about technology per se." This is a fundamental issue that has repeatedly surfaced in this book. Initial attempts at using visual media in worship at Union-Congregational Church included a cycle of planning, feedback, evaluation, and "back to the drawing board" experimentation. A computer, LCD projector, and presentation software eventually became the delivery method of choice because they were easy to use. People in the congregation who wanted to continue the media-enhanced worship opportunity gave generously to secure the needed equipment.

The handful of people who met at the front of the sanctuary in the chancel slowly grew into a group of twenty, then thirty people. Within a year forty, then fifty people began attending. Multimedia worship went from an experiment to a regular opportunity for a new experience of worship that was engaging people where they lived.

The ministry continued to flourish, not because the technological advances were powerful (though they were), but because the pastor and the people continued to seek ways to reach out to people who sought meaning for their lives but had not discovered that meaning through traditional worship environments. A highlight in the program was the multimedia Easter service in 2002, when attendance was more than the two traditional services combined.

Bringing about a new ministry of outreach has not been without difficulty. Barriers have been encountered and dealt with. Preferred styles of worship have been discussed and debated. Mission has been examined, evaluated, and agonized over. But again, the keys to success have been (1) pastoral leadership that encourages collegial ministry and (2) lay leadership entrusted with freedom to dialogue, debate, and develop ministry opportunities. The result has been success in creating a healthy, inviting, and open place where God can do a *new thing* in the midst of his people. Technology is helpful, and people who are skilled in technology are a wonderful addition to the ministry team. But technology comes in a distant third when compared to competent and open pastoral leadership and lay persons who are empowered for ministry.

A Thanksgiving Service

It is the Sunday before Thanksgiving when I pull into the parking lot of Union-Congregational Church. Finding my way into the sanctuary, I am impressed by the number of people who have gathered. People in casual dress are beginning to fill the sanctuary and the mood is relaxed. There are older people, children, teenagers, and a number of families sitting together. Most surprising is the twenty- and thirty-somethings who are normally missing from Sunday mornings in most mainline churches. As the time for worship approaches, I am reading through a simple bulletin that has a take-home version of the announcements and an outline of the service and communion prayers. The first item in the announcements stands out, "11:20 A.M. Seminary Student Advisory Committee." A full-time seminary student on a year-long internship is assigned to the congregation, and lay people are very much invested in her year-long time of learning with them. The message seems to emerge from every aspect of the church's life—"We are a community that shares a ministry, not a church that has a few professional ministers."

Quiet, contemporary music comes through the speakers and images with a Thanksgiving theme fill the screen at the front of the sanctuary. Some of the images show fields and crops around the town. Interspersed with the images are announcements for the day. There will be Holy Communion today, and the Lord's Table is set with bread, wine, and candles. The colors on the table, in the images, and even in the lighting seem to have been planned. (When I inquired about this after the service, a team member explained, "Yes, *everything* is planned.")

The pastor steps to the front of the sanctuary and explains that today's theme is Thanksgiving and that we will be thinking together about what thanksgiving means to us, to our families, and to our relationship with God. There is a time of greeting one other, and then we join in an opening prayer that is projected on the screen. A unison Scripture brings us together around the theme of giving and thanksgiving:

> You will be enriched in every way for your great generosity, which will
> produce thanksgiving to God through us; for the rendering of this ministry
> not only supplies the needs of the saints but also overflows with many
> thanksgivings to God. (2 Cor. 9:11–12)

The pastor begins to talk about the traditions and rituals that make
up our lives. Thanksgiving is one of those traditions, and most of us
do not like change when it comes to our cherished customs. For the
pastor, Thanksgiving Day is not Thanksgiving Day without sweet potatoes baked with a little brown sugar and those golden baked mini-
marshmallows on top. Now a clip from the movie *Escanaba in Da
Moonlight* begins. Four men are on their annual deer hunting trip
in Upper Michigan. As they get ready to head into the fields, one of
the men remarks that he cannot wait for dinner when they have their
pasties. The pasty is a time-honored meal, and any self-respecting citi-
zen of the Upper Peninsula, otherwise known as "Yoopers," could tell
you that a pasty has beef, potatoes, onion, rutabaga, and turnip baked
inside a golden crust. Cornish miners and their wives are properly
given the credit for bringing the pasty to the Upper Peninsula in the
early 1850s, when the copper and iron mines were first being opened.
The pasty has been described as "a hearty and hot, hand-held meal
for miners who had no time to come above ground for lunch. Some
miners reheated their pasties underground; others kept them at least
body warm in a chest pocket. Others set their pasties on a mining
shovel and held them over head-lamp candles until warmed."[6]
    The film clip begins at a point where one of the men tells the others
that they are not going to have pasties at deer camp this year. "I thought
we would try something different," he said. This brings the world to a
screeching halt as a heated discussion ensues. There is a hint from one
of the men who is holding his rifle that the offending party might suffer
some violence if there are indeed no pasties at deer camp. "Change is
good," the man continues. At this point, his brother begins a long recita-
tion of how everything about deer camp is the same year after year. He
wears the same shirt every year, drives the same pickup truck to camp,
uses the same gun and ammunition, and has pasties for supper. And he
always gets a deer. That's what deer camp is all about, and it can't be
deer camp if anything is changed—especially pasties for supper.[7] The

clip is right on target as many in the congregation chuckle and nod their heads in agreement. Change is difficult.

"At one level," the pastor says as the film clip fades, "rituals seem to be ridiculous as the clip shows, yet they connect us with family and bring to mind all kinds of memories that are important to us." He goes on to talk about how it is that Thanksgiving is a time when these rituals and traditions are important for families, and especially for the family we belong to as the community of faith. The Greek word for thanksgiving, *eucharist*, he explains is what some traditions use for communion. The pastor goes to the table and lifts up the bread and a cup of wine and tells us that this is the Thanksgiving table for Christian people. Our traditions and rituals here take us back hundreds of years and connect us with the great family of faith of all ages. Traditions bind us to family, and our Christian rituals call to mind the love that brought Christ to earth to bring us all into the presence of God.

At this point, the pastor sits as the song, "Love Will Keep Us Alive," by the Eagles[5] is played as a PowerPoint presentation with words and images shown. One of the members of the high school youth group has prepared this presentation; it is her first time to participate. Some of her friends have come with her to see her work. Many of the images used in the presentation are of people in the congregation. There are young people, older people, and then a picture of a young person in the church standing alone in a field just outside of town. The words are, "I was standing all alone against the world outside." Then there are images of people joined together in fellowship in Sunday school, in the youth group, and at a senior gathering. The images are generating new meanings for familiar words, "Lost and lonely, Now you've given me the will to survive, When we're hungry . . . love will keep us alive." Some are singing along, and it is clear that there are some 1970s people around who know the music of the Eagles well. There are misty eyes and a few tears here and there as people are reflecting on the love of family, friends, and the fellowship of faith that brings deep meaning to our lives. New connections are being made as the music, images, and meaning of people's lives are ushered into the larger meaning of God's love, which has come to us in Christ. Although the words from the song, "Now I've found you, there's no more emptiness inside . . ." had to do with romantic love in the Eagles' song, the message easily translates to the discovery of the love of Christ, which has brought this community together. The music and art of our cultural experiences bear deep meaning for living and integration of these expressions into the experience of worship. New pathways for the gospel message to be received are being opened week by week.

The pastor now moves to the table once again and speaks of the love of Christ, which in the deepest spiritual sense makes us and keeps us alive. He gathers the elements of the experience together as our traditions have prepared a way to appreciate anew the great tradition of Holy Communion, and thanksgiving is connected with the Great Thanksgiving of Eucharist. We are invited to come to the table and receive the bread and wine. Music plays as a beautiful collection of artwork depicting the Last Supper is projected. Our thoughts are drawn to the greatest gift of all as we reflect on the artistic interpretation of Holy Communion by artists and photographers. The technology does not intrude. There are no wires, no computers visible, and no LCD projector with its electronic whispers. This is not an imitation of an Imax theatre.[9] The communion table is central, the worshipers are engaged, and the images are natural and nourishing. I am personally drawn into the mystery of the gift of Christ by Salvador Dali's *The Last Supper*. As we are dismissed with a blessing, I join in the greetings and sense a joyful reflective spirit.

A question is answered. Can technology be used in something so sacred as Holy Communion without intruding horribly? The technology has been transparent. There has been a feast of sight, song, and image. It is as though we have seen some of the great stained glass art of medieval cathedrals, except that these collections are more than one could hope for in a single cathedral. With the rest of the congregation, I find myself closer to my own traditions, which even includes my "Yooper" father, aunts, uncles, and grandparents. And I find myself understanding just a bit more of the power of my spiritual traditions. I am thankful.

Why Are They Coming?

After worship, most of the congregation stayed to enjoy coffee and conversation. The conversation was essentially a continuation of the things that were experienced during worship. People shared memories of traditions and rituals that were important to families. Moms and dads in their late thirties and forties talked about the music that was a part of their younger years. Teens gathered around their friend who had just finished her first presentation for worship. The most amazing thing was that most of these people were not a part of this church three years ago.

Many of the people were anxious to share their experience with me. They were excited about discovering a new way of worshiping and being part of the church. One young man in his late twenties said that his spiritual journey began almost three years ago when he first visited the multimedia service. Until that time, his wife attended church, but he did not. The church holds a combined service once a month when everyone gathers for a more traditional worship and Communion is served. "I don't come to that one," the young man said, "but otherwise, I never miss." He said that he never imagined that he would attend church every week. "The pastor sent out a survey," he volunteered. "He wanted to know if we found the service entertaining. He's concerned that we not just entertain people, but I'm not so sure that's all bad." He went on to say that part of the reason he comes is that the things going on in worship relate to his daily living. "Some of the entertaining moments are the parts that have me thinking about the message during the week." The entertainment he experiences is not so much the kind of entertainment where one leaves a movie when the screen says, "The End." This experience gets the worshiper's attention, but the end result is a connection with their lives and the world they live in.

Another young woman relates a common spiritual journey. She was raised in a tradition that is anything but participatory and dropped out when she went to college. A friend told her about this ministry, and she came with her husband and children. They come as a family and feel welcomed and comfortable with people who are on the same life journey as they are. "The approach and the message speak to me in ways I've never experienced before," she said.

One last conversation I had was with two couples who have been attending this service for just about three years. The story is similar to that of many of the people who have become a part of the church through this multimedia worship service. They were not active in any church and only loosely related to the religious traditions of their families of origin. They had no particular guilt about not being a part of organized religion and were comfortable passing along family values and morals without the benefit of the organized church. They came to this church through the greatest evangelism program of all time. Friends told them about the service and invited them to visit. The leadership of this church does not hammer away at the congregation with the "Bring a friend to church with you next week" speech. They know very well that people who discover things that bring meaning and value to their lives will share the experience with people they know and care about. When we have to tell, ask, or beg people in our churches to "bring a friend," the game has already been lost. One of the young fathers I was talking with said it quite clearly, "If Jim (the friend who had invited him) was taking his family to church, I knew something remarkable was going on here." He said that he keeps coming back because the message always connects with his reality.

Behind the Scenes

Before I headed back to Highway 151 for the return drive home where I would unpack this experience in my mind, I sat down with two leaders of the planning team that meets weekly to put this service together.[10] They shared a few essential principles that guide the creation of their worship services.

- Team Process: Every multimedia service arrives at a Sunday morning only after the planning team has put together the theme, music, images, and message. The pastor and team meet together every week to study Scripture, explore themes, discuss music and visual resources, and appoint persons to the various tasks that will be needed in creating the experience.
- Thematic Integrity: Everything that takes place in the service is examined in light of the team's work with a theme. In many Protestant congregations, it is as though the worship is put together with Scotch tape and Post-it notes. An award is presented, the Sunday school class sings a song, someone who is visiting worship with friends happens to have a great voice and a quick

solo is arranged, or the choir has worked hard on a particular anthem and wants to sing it at all the morning services. The team at Waupun spends a good deal of time working through every aspect of the service. From time to time someone will come up with an idea, a song, or a desire to add something to the worship experience, but the criteria is that the service be woven together with thematic integrity. Nothing is added that does not fit with the theme. The resulting experience is a single coherent theme that connects with the worshipers. "The music and visuals bring people back to church during the week," one of the team leaders points out. "This week they will see and hear things that will bring the thanksgiving theme to mind, and it brings them back to church." By insisting on a focused concentration and working hard on building a worship experience, the community is not only growing in numbers, it is growing in numbers of people who are more intentionally thinking about spiritual-theological issues in their living. Life-building, community-enhancing connections are being woven together in the fabric of their disconnected worlds.

- Total Community Involvement: There is no solo ministry at Union-Congregational Church. The work of the worship team is enhanced by the growing number of people who bring ideas, photographs, theological questions, and ideas for new themes. It has been a joy for the pastor to see people from young to old who look for biblical themes in music, movies, art, and the world around them. One of the team leaders is a school psychologist with a keen interest in developmental issues, learning styles, and how faith is communicated for our culture. Rather, he *now* has a keen interest. Until the multimedia worship experience came along, he was very nominally connected with church. "I used to attend infrequently, and when I did, I was calculating what swing I might use to make a putt down the aisle if the cup were at the front."[11] He once came to the planning group with an idea for using a *Star Wars* clip. The pastor said, "Why don't you do the message?" He not only did the *Star Wars* service, he is preparing a theme called "Quantum Religion" based on quantum theory and the movie *The Power of Ten*. He plans to address the issue of how God is involved at the tiniest places in our lives. "There is mystery *out there*," he said, "but there is also mystery and wonder *in here*." In this process, the saints are indeed being equipped for the work of ministry.

- Technological Transparency: As we talked, it was clear that the technology behind all of this was secondary. There are technical issues like brand of software, rear screen projection, operating sound and computer systems, and coordinating the presentations. But little of our talk was about the technology. It was clear that technology enabled the multimedia worship; however, "It's mainly the message isn't it?" I observed. The response was immediate—"It's **all** about the message!" One additional aspect of using technology in the multimedia worship is important for most churches. "*We allow it to be human,*" a team leader says. "*We make mistakes now and then. The song doesn't cue up or a slide is in the wrong order . . . and we laugh.*" It isn't a matter of being sloppy. The group plans, rehearses, evaluates, and takes great care with the use of technology. But, it is not perfect, and they are representative of the majority of churches that will make significant progress in the cities, towns, and countryside of the American Christian landscape. This team is not looking for the slick, polished professional presentation that is much more vulnerable to crossing the line into mere entertainment.

Three historic issues in local church ministry are addressed in a natural way through the multimedia worship experience at Union-Congregational Church. They were not specifically a part of the conversations in developing the media ministry, but the resulting ministry has clearly made a difference in leadership, evangelism, and preaching. Leadership is taught and "caught" as the community embraces the worship service as "our" ministry. There are very few passive spectators in this environment. Most are involved in bringing friends and bringing ideas, and sooner or later, most will hear from the pastor, "Why don't you do that?" The evangelism occurs naturally as people continue to share with family and friends how their lives are being touched. As for preaching, it is clear that the team is doing the work of exegeting Scripture, but more than that, they are exegeting the congregation and proclaiming the message in the venues where people live.

The story of Union-Congregational Church is in part a story of how the use of digital technology can enhance evangelism ministry. We turn now to the issue of eVangelism, or how digital technologies can enhance the evangelism ministry of the church.

eVangelism—Digital Tools for Growing the Church

Here . . . then is a great new art which has laid hold of all classes of people . . . wisdom would seem to direct that the Church cooperate in its development and utilize it in every possible way . . . in reaching the unchurched masses.[1]

Orrin G. Cocks (On the use of film in church, 1916)

Digital technology has remarkable potential for evangelism. It provides the possibility of knocking on every door in a community without the disadvantage of turning people off. Quality brochures can be produced for less than one dollar each. Hundreds of personal contacts with people who have interest in your ministry can be accomplished in an evening's work. One of the marvelous things about digital technologies is the ability to reach out in inviting, nonthreatening ways that allow persons to choose inquiry. Technology sensitively integrated in ministry can provide a genuinely seeker-sensitive venue for exploration of Christian faith. In order to take advantage of the promise of these tools for the church's work of evangelism, there is a process that should be engaged. Framing an approach to using technology in evangelism using the concepts of message, mission, and method will insure more productive results. Each concept represents homework that will need to be faithfully done.

Message, Mission, and Method

Message: "What, exactly, is it you want to say?" The very first task of any group's outreach program is to identify and clarify what it is that is being offered. In purely secular marketing terms, evangelism is trying to sell something religious in an oversold market to people who have no particular desire for the product. That is to say, everybody in America has heard the pitch, and there should be little argument about the fact that America is a pagan nation.

I use the term pagan in a loving way. Many of the people I love most are pagans. I use the term to refer to people who choose to live their lives without reference to God. They can be wonderful, moral people who contribute greatly to society. Their choice of life without God is not a judgment about whether they are decent persons. The same holds true for our pagan culture. This is a culture that is tolerant of religion, ill disposed to Christianity, and much like the Athens that Paul found tolerant of, but mostly immune to, his gospel. "All the Athenians and the foreigners who lived there spent their time doing nothing but talking about and listening to the latest ideas" (Acts 17:21). The spiritual wanderlust of ancient Athens is alive and well in our culture.

It will take more than a church sign at the curb proclaiming, "Everybody Welcome" to reach this generation. The congregation or ministry group needs a clear expression of the message it proposes to bring to a pagan world. This will take more than self-study or time of visioning or revisioning that is aimed at producing a "mission statement." A search on Google using the search terms "church mission statement" produced thousands of hits. It appears that producing mission statements is a favorite pastime of churches of every conceivable Christian communion these days. After looking through the first 100 pages of links to church mission statements, it was clear the world could be changed by tomorrow night if all the love, acceptance, forgiveness, fellowship, and caring for all persons expressed in the mission statements would be actualized tomorrow morning. The essential point here is that a church or ministry's message has to be concise, easily understood, believable, and clearly manifested in the actual life of the group.

Why is this initial step so important? Simple. The most sophisticated website in the world or the greatest CD brochure in the country will be of no value if the message is not relevant and effective. Technology cannot turn a poorly conceived message into a successful outreach. Imagine a church with a sign at the curb that lists worship hours and in bold letters proclaims, "Visitors Welcome." It's a nice gesture, but probably no more appealing than a sign over a fast food joint that says, "Hamburgers." A church down the street has a similar sign, only it reads, "Everybody Welcome." This is better. It is somewhat analogous to "Really Good Hamburgers." Finally, there is a church with a sign that declares "Absolutely Anyone Welcome Here—Really!" This *might* speak to spiritually hungry folks like a sign over a restaurant that proclaims "Hamburgers To Die For!"

Take some time with the primary question. What exactly is the message you want to deliver? "Visitors Welcome" and "Absolutely Anyone Welcome Here—Really!" are radically different. What are those differences and what do they mean? Which comes closest to your own situation? Imagine that you have an opportunity to tell your story in a very short paragraph to a pagan who is suspicious of, but open to, your message. What do you come up with that is an honest reflection of who you are as a congregation or ministry and the message you have to offer? Once a clear message is identified the next step can be taken.

Mission: Who exactly do you want to reach? Once the message is clarified, the essential next step is to know who the message is being directed toward. This is the "missional direction" of your work. An unchurched audience of young families is different from a group of denominationally connected families who are seeking a church of their family background. A minority ethnic community requires a completely different approach from an upper-middle-class group of Anglo teenagers. When the message has been clarified and is appropriate for the missional direction of the church, the method or methods of sharing or delivering the message can be selected.

Method: There are multiple ways digital tools can assist in bringing the message to a particular group. Print media such as newspapers, direct mail, and yellow pages have provided the primary tools for reaching out to traditional groups. Even with the addition of digital tools such as websites, print media will continue to play a role in pointing people to your message. Nevertheless, Internet usage continues to grow, and an Internet demographic study of your target group is one of the basic tools that should be used in developing a delivery strategy. Seventy-five percent of young people 14 to 17 years old go online.[2] If reaching families is a priority, using Web-based resources and e-mail will be important considerations. While minority and ethnic groups have lagged behind the white population in Internet use, this is changing. The Latino community is one of the fastest growing populations going online. Seniors are also a fast growing segment of the Internet population.[3] All of this means that Web-based ministry, e-mail, use of CD-based brochures, and Internet-based interactivity will become increasingly important tools for the church's ministry of evangelism.

Before addressing some specific ways a church might choose to use digital resources in evangelism, I want to take you to a brief bit of history related to evangelism and media that illustrates one of the major concepts of this book. Namely, technology works well as a servant of ministry, but poorly as a sole solution for ministry.

Motion Pictures—A Chance to Save the World with New Technology?

The turn of the twentieth century brought a new technology to the public arena. People across the country were captivated by the "moving picture." Although the relationship between Hollywood and the church was destined for trouble, it was not always so with some people in the church.

Literary Digest published an article in 1916 entitled, "Urging an Alliance of Church and Motion Picture."[4] The article quoted Orrin G. Cocks, advisory secretary to the National Board of Censorship of the Protestant Episcopal Church, as saying, "The motion picture has demonstrated in scores of cities and towns that it has a more powerful hold upon the men than has the saloon. Liquor licenses are falling off, the corner saloon is disappearing, sobriety in the home of workingmen is supplanting the waste of character. . . ."[5] Another magazine article from 1916 attributes the transformation of a small town in western New York to the sophisticated use of film technology. Reverend Harry E. Robbins mobilized a men's club. He proceeded to rent an opera house, purchase motion picture equipment, and open a theater. Tickets to the movies were given to children, choir members, and others who would attend Sunday school, sing in the choir, and otherwise participate in wholesome and community-building activities. Community leaders testified that Rev. Robbins's use of the movie house was literally responsible for a positive transformation of the community.[6]

History documents, of course, that the church did not use film to eliminate alcoholism or transform whole communities. The technology that changed the entertainment industry did not turn out to be the culture-transforming silver bullet some predicted. The use of film in churches did not save the world after all, and it would be toward the end of the century before film would once again have a place in the life of the church through multimedia ministry such as that of Union-Congregational Church in Waupun, Wisconsin. As a tool, film may once again play a part in reaching out to our generation. This time around, those who use film wisely will realize that the medium has great potential, but it does not have an inherent power to advance the mission of the church.

Digital Tools for eVangelism

Once a message is identified and a missional direction chosen, appropriate digital tools can provide powerful outreach abilities. One possibility for use of the tools is what I call a "parachute drop." A church planter goes to a community to begin a ministry from scratch. The basic message the new church wants to deliver is that "this church will provide a place where absolutely anyone is welcome. Our worship style is informal, nontraditional, and celebrative. We are especially anxious to welcome people who have no church background at all, or who have dropped out of church altogether." The missional direction of the infant church targets a population of younger families with children who are not active in church. The atmosphere will be casual and nonliturgical. Music will be contemporary; worship will include multimedia experiences; and the preaching ministry will focus on simple, biblically based teaching on marriage, family, and contemporary themes for people whose vocabulary does not include traditional theological concepts like redemption, justification, sanctification, or eschatology. (Not that many folks do have such a vocabulary anymore.)

The approach of the church planter is to arrive in town and begin the task of getting acquainted with people in the community, participating in community activities, and volunteering at the local elementary school. He gathers personal e-mail addresses as the digital gems that they are. A website is prepared that includes the basic message and missional direction of the church and takes the format of an informative newsletter while the developmental work for the new church is being done. E-mail newsletters are sent out to a growing list of addresses. The e-mail is very carefully worded to offer an "opt-out" for anyone who does not want to receive the electronic mail. Using good e-mail etiquette, all e-mail sent by the church will include an up-front apology to anyone who receives the e-mail unsolicited. With an increasing volume of spam flooding people's e-mail inboxes, sending unsolicited e-mail is quickly taking the place of insensitive, "in your face" witnessing. Every opportunity is taken to point people to the website and secure permissions to send e-mail messages. A business card with a carefully worded slogan such as, "With us, absolutely everyone is welcome," is passed out to absolutely everyone who will accept it. An extra is always included "for a friend." The business card includes the church website address. Two newspaper ads, not in the religion section, highlight the church's basic message and also include the Web address. The website of the gathering congregation contains extensive information for those who wish to learn more about the group. As inquirers begin to show more than passing interest, casual home group conversations take place and the congregation moves toward a hopeful beginning.

This process is the story of more than one congregation in which simple digital tools are used in its development. The Bridge Christian Church in Dubuque, Iowa, used many of these tools effectively. Combined with a solid grasp of its message and clear understanding of its missional directive, they were able to make good use of the digital tools they chose.[7] Sixteen months after the church's senior minister and church planter arrived, the church held its first worship service with 155 persons in attendance.

Beyond the Basics

There are additional possibilities that can be used by church planters or existing churches seeking ways to enhance evangelistic outreach.

Web Ministry: A Web ministry can include interactive features like those discussed in the work of the hypothetical First Church Online. The opportunity to interact with leadership from a congregation prior to any commitment to attend worship can help people make the transition from inquirer to visitor less painful.

A superb way to reach out to people who are searching for spiritual community, but are also very unsure about their beliefs, is the approach of Ruth Tucker, who wrote the book *Walking Away From Faith.*[8] Tucker reaches out to people who are questioning their faith through the website Questioning Faith.[9] People can bring their questions to the website and count on a personal response. This offers a completely nonthreatening way for people to express their doubts and difficulties. This site provides a model that could be used by local churches. Each church should fashion its approach according to their own theological and missional style. This project will require a major commitment from a person who will lead this section of ministry. Another example of how an outreach like this can work is on the website of our First Church Online. Visit the discussion center of the site and then the topic, "Got Faith?" Once this ministry is active, word of mouth and print advertising can be used to drive traffic to this outreach.

Three websites make my "must visit" list for those who will use the Internet as a part of their evangelism program. The first is a website for those who plan and author the website for your group. There is a myriad of resources and advanced help through the Christian Webmasters Association website.[10] This online resource is a place to share tips, knowledge, code for advanced functionality, and more. The second is the online evangelism website sponsored by Gospelcom.net.[11] The site is aimed at a theologically conservative audience, but the resources can be used or modified by any group that wants to reach out with Internet ministry. This site makes my "must visit" list because of its extensive resources for devotional life, free downloads for your PDA (such as Palm Pilot), Christian history resources, and Bible study resources. The third and last site is a resource for those who work with young people in the church, Youth Specialties.[12] Commitment to youth ministry in today's cultural climate is fundamental to success in evangelism. The Youth Specialties site is worth a visit if for no other reason than its list of 100 tips and tricks for youth leaders.

Digital Brochures: A website or e-mail newsletter can be used to promote a CD people can request be mailed to them. A CD can hold an amazing amount of material. Using video clips in the CD brochure can bring a personal touch to persons who may be searching for a church, or simply searching for spiritual meaning. The increasing availability of tools for creating DVD movies will become a staple in outreach ministry in the next two years. "Seeing" the pastor as opposed to just reading the pastor's welcome will effectively personalize your ministry without threatening the seeker. Short interviews with people who match your target audience will be especially valuable. Inexpensive software is available for conversion of VHS tapes to digital format for CD.[13] For those who do not have the desire to learn video editing, there are inexpensive services available that will convert VHS footage to digital format for you.

The great advantage of CD brochures is that they can be produced for less than one dollar per copy and they hold more information than an average textbook.

Business Cards: Mini compact disks serve as digital business cards. These CDs are an amazing tool, with a wide array of applications. A business-card-sized CD can hold up to 50MB of information. These small cards can also hold audio and video files. They are the size of a business card and easy for members of your group to carry for giving to friends and neighbors. Consider sending these mini CDs or even the standard CD to a targeted zip code to evaluate response. Links can be placed on the disk so that as people are reading the disk on their computer, they are able to connect directly with your church website or send e-mail inquiries from their computer.

The CD format is appealing to people who use a home computer and the Internet. While most people throw bulk mail away, computer users and particularly younger populations are likely to pop a CD into their disk drive out of curiosity.

Last Words About eVangelism

As with every other aspect of ministry and technology, the key issue in evangelism is the people of the local congregation more than it is the technology. Technology offers important new tools, but the people are the context in which God's action takes place. Behind every good church website, and all the promises of warm welcomes and relevant teaching that come via digital technologies, there must an authentic group of people bound together in commitment to bring the good news of God's reign in our lives and in our world. The key to success is found in a line borrowed from the customer service folks: "Promise less than you can deliver and deliver more than you promise."

The field of technology is a growing, changing, sometimes frustrating, and ever-moving target. The need to communicate the Good News, however, is the unchanging directive in this changing culture. It is time to bring together the promise and the possibilities of technology with the potential of the ancient Good News of God for our world. The times call for strong leaders who are connected. What does it mean to be a "connected" Christian leader?

The Connected Christian Leader

. . . whenever a baby is born anywhere in the world, he is given at birth a number which will be his telephone number for life. As soon as he can talk, he is given a watchlike device with 10 little buttons on one side and a screen on the other. Thus equipped, at any time when he wishes to talk with anyone in the world, he will pull out the device and punch on the keys the number of his friend.[1]

Dr. Harold Osborne

The Price of Connectivity

Theresa Turner was one of the most connected people in the town where I grew up. She was one of the operators at "central" (the telephone company's central switching station), and by virtue of her job, was as good as a daily newspaper. In all likelihood she knew as much about everyone in town as anyone around. Operators were not supposed to listen in on people's conversations, but most people knew better than to talk about personal issues over the telephone. The operators in our town were the original "Caller ID." The technology was simple. All you had to do was ask an operator if Dick Jones had called the bank today, and she would answer something like, "No, but Tom over at the bank called Dick last Friday."

Jimmy Turner was my best friend in grade school, and we would talk on the telephone almost every day. I still remember Jimmy's phone number. I would pick up the receiver, put it up to my ear, and give the crank on the side of the box a quick turn. The operator would answer, "Number please?" "324J," I would reply, and after a few short rings Jimmy would answer the phone.

On one particular day, Jimmy and I were talking and making plans for our Saturday. He suggested we go down to his dad's boat house and take out the 12-foot fishing dingy with the nifty, new 7½ horsepower Johnson outboard. "Jimmy!" A female voice interrupted our call with a serious scolding, "You know very well your daddy doesn't want you out in that boat without him!"[2]

Even in those days, it turns out, technology has always come with problems. Back then, a phone call was for someone in our family if there were two short rings. Occasionally I would listen in on Beverly Watson's conversations by picking up a moment or two after one short and one long ring. Mrs. Cooper (who was two long rings) picked up on just about everyone's conversations. She was a lonely widow and television had not yet come to northern Ontario. The party line telephone was her major source of entertainment. I can remember my father saying from time to time, "Mrs. Cooper, you hang up that phone now. This call is for me."

Invasion of privacy and assault on personal boundaries is a persistent dilemma that comes in the wake of technological advances. The desire for convenience and connection will usually win out over the loss of privacy in our choices. From the earliest telephones connected by party lines to contemporary cell phones, the desire to be connected is a driving force in human existence. The price of all this connectivity is erosion of our privacy and a blurring of our personal boundaries. Mrs. Cooper's not so subtle snooping has been replaced by sophisticated listening equipment that can snatch your cell phone conversations from the air. The price of progress is not limited to loss of privacy. There is an insidious way in which technology has placed many Christian leaders in a kind of digital bondage. Many of us can be reached anytime and anywhere by cell phone, pager, fax, or e-mail. All of this *reachability* implies *availability*. A Verizon television commercial showing a man tramping about remote locations shouting, "Can you hear me now?" points to a time when wireless networking will literally cover the world. Unless Christian leaders use great caution and personal discipline, the days of any solitude could well be over.

Harold Osborne missed the mark with his 1954 prediction of a personal lifelong telephone number, but he was right on target in believing that the telephone would have an enormous sociological impact on our world. He knew that our connections would come to be very important in our lives. However, I shudder to think who might be calling if I had a phone number today that had been assigned to me the day I was born. I have expressed no little concern in this book over the dangers of inappropriate imposition of technology on the life of the church. In the time it has taken to develop and write this manuscript, the situation has continued to grow worse. Religious cyberlitter continues on an upward spiral and growing numbers of sanctuaries are cluttered with computers, wires, and projectors. In a presentation to pastors on what it means to be a connected Christian leader, I expressed the opinion that 98 percent of all church websites should be closed. Some did not like hearing this. The most vociferous reactions reminded me of Wall Street analyst Susan Kalla's experience when she criticized Wall Street ways that have failed. "Nobody likes it when you tell them their children are ugly," she said.[3] Some church leaders *really* do not like it when you tell them their digital children (websites) are ugly.

The Basis of Authentic Connection

Despite the misuse of technology and problems related to digital connectivity, there are some ways to ensure that the connections we make are authentic. The truly connected Christian leader who will have an impact in our disconnected world is theologically grounded, spiritually centered, and technologically informed. The latter has value only when the former two characteristics are in place. These connections determine whether a person can lead a community in the successful integration of new technologies in a theologically and spiritually healthy way. The health of our ministry through technology will depend on a threefold hierarchy of connections: (1) connection with God, (2) connection with the community, and (3) connection with information.

- *Connection with God*: Unless the leader is firmly connected in a relationship with God and growing in disciplines of the Christian faith, no other connections or connectivity will have value for the kingdom of God. The peace of Christ alone is the peace that can counter the urgent and sometimes chaotic world of technology. Jesus said, "Peace I leave with you; my peace I give to you. I do not give to you as the world gives" (John 14:27). A truly connected Christian leader will be one for whom the peace of Christ is the personal and community foundation that supports the promise of technology.

- *Connection with the community*: As the connected Christian leader is grounded in a healthy relationship with God, so he or she will have a deep commitment to and connection with the body of Christ. The leader understands that the role of those who have been called and gifted to serve the family of faith is "to equip the saints for the work of ministry" (Eph. 4:12). The Christian leader's genuine connection with the community of faith is a visible authentication of the connection with God.

- *Connection with information*: Finally, a critical ingredient of ministry is information. Information about God and knowledge of God are essential to a relationship with God. The writer of 1 Timothy says that God our Savior "desires everyone to be saved and to come to the knowledge of the truth" (1 Tim. 2:4). Christians are encouraged to "grow in the grace and knowledge of our Lord and Savior Jesus Christ" (2 Peter 3:18). In the most fundamental sense, the Christian leader is under the call of God to bring the information or the facts about Jesus Christ to the world in a way that will enable persons to come to the knowledge of God.

As the Internet and e-mail provide us with growing opportunities to pass on information, there is a corollary need to communicate thoughtfully, prayerfully, and judiciously. In the Sermon on the Mount, Jesus said, "When you are praying, do not heap up empty phrases as the Gentiles do; for they think that they will be heard because of their many words" (Matt. 6:7). Were Jesus to address his digitally literate followers today, he might say something like, "Do not flood the world with information as the heathens do, for they think they will be heard because of their massive data."

Essentials of Connection

The savvy Christian leader in our time understands that technology is here to stay. Church members and their children are saturated in a digital world, and technological literacy is essential for effective leadership. Basic skills in the understanding and use of information technologies will facilitate personal, professional, and community growth. It is not possible to know everything about technologies that have potential for ministry—indeed, it would be poor stewardship to spend an inordinate amount of time in strictly technological pursuits, but the following three areas provide the essentials. As you read through these areas, the endnotes will take you to specific websites that provide additional information.

Basic Tools

The foundation for all use of new technologies is basic computer literacy. Most people have basic computer knowledge, access to the Internet, and the ability to use e-mail.[4] For those who do not, purchase of a computer, connecting to the Internet, and setting up an e-mail account is a necessary first task. When the computer is set up, access to the Internet is gained, and e-mail is activated, the next step will be to learn to navigate the Internet and use e-mail. Over half the population in the United States now uses the Internet, 75 percent of young people between the ages of 14–17 are online, and between 2000 and 2002, e-mail use jumped from 35 percent to 45 percent within the population. Use of the Internet in rural areas grew slowly, but by February of 2001, rural populations had caught up to the national average in Internet usage.[5] Christian leaders who do not have access to the Internet or e-mail (e-mail is the most popular use of the Internet) will be increasingly out of touch with most of the people in their faith community. While it is not necessary for Christian leaders to become cyberspace cadets, the online experience *is* a part of our common parlance today and leaders must have basic knowledge of the field.

At a minimum, the Christian leader is computer literate, has Internet access, and is familiar with the use of e-mail. But this is a minimum. It is the equivalent of taking a brief course in conversational French in preparation for a trip to Paris. The course will help with finding a hotel, taking a taxi ride, and ordering breakfast. It will not, however, prepare one for life in France. True leadership in the family of faith in ministry and technology requires more than a traveler's acquaintance with digital conversation.

In the case of young people in the church, it is unthinkable that someone who works with teens would not be familiar with the virtual world. In fact, our youth leaders should be asked to have skill with digital technology and the Internet, *including Internet games.* The youth leader's repertoire has grown from softball, ping pong, camping, and roller skating to the point where it should include online gaming. Leaders cannot model responsible use of the Internet and online gaming for entertainment if they are not familiar with the medium.

Personal Tools

Most people who hold leadership positions in the Christian community have been using the Internet and e-mail to advantage for some time. The Internet has become a source of personal enrichment through websites like *The Daily Office*, which has the daily lectionary passages as well as the complete daily office of the Anglican Communion.[6] The website Universalis has similar resources for Roman Catholic leaders.[7] One of the largest Christian resources on the Internet is Gospelcom.net (www.gospelcom.net), where there is a daily devotional resource called "Our Daily Bread." This site also includes links to Scripture passages organized to read through the Bible in a year. The passages are also available as audio files.[8]

One of the more powerful tools available is the PDA, or Personal Digital Assistant. PDAs offer the opportunity to break the paper habit. Instead of paper calendar organizers, the PDA keeps a calendar, address and phone book, expense log, calculator, and memo pad. There is an alarm that can be set as a reminder of important dates or appointments. The PDA comes with an interface to the desktop computer, allowing for backup of all data. Data can also be entered directly to the computer and downloaded to the PDA, and when the user is not at the computer, data can be directly entered on the PDA with a stylus.

Another helpful application of the PDA is the ability to download e-mail from the computer and read, reply to, or forward the e-mail. The next time one logs on to the computer, all the e-mail activity is uploaded to the e-mail program and sent, forwarded, or deleted according to the stored instructions. For just a few more dollars, a folding keyboard is available. The PDA and keyboard fit in a small case the size of a Bible. For personal enrichment in those times when you are waiting in the doctor's office, delayed in traffic, or stuck on a long layover at the airport, the PDA can provide reading material. It is possible to have everything from *The Book of Common Prayer*, to Calvin's *Institutes*, to a Bible program set up to read the Bible through in a year.[9] And *all* of this is available with an entry level PDA. Prices have dropped considerably, and the functionality of this small device will quickly earn a place in your most valued time management and convenience resources.[10]

A nice surprise I discovered early on with my PDA is the ability to search its database to find specific names, notes, or memos. The search term will find every occurrence of the term in the calendar, memos, address book, or entire books that have been downloaded. This would provide an instant concordance with a search of the Bible on the PDA. Advanced use of the search function can cross reference texts. Calvin's *Institutes* and a Bible text can be searched in a way that provides a cross-reference study between the two.

The initial transition from a paper-based calendar to a PDA comes with a bit of withdrawal. I kept both a Day-Timer calendar and ap-pointment book *and* my PDA for a month as I learned to trust my digital device. What if the batteries fell out of my PDA and I lost all my data? (They did!) The moral of *this* story is to always save your files! One of my mantras for the digital era is "BUSB," or, "Back up, stupid, back up!"

Professional Tools

As the Christian leader becomes more comfortable with the digital environment, a new and growing world of digital resources becomes a significant source of professional growth. Our discussion of the PDA barely scratched the surface of the effective resources beginning to emerge from the research and development of this powerful little device. Prices continue to fall and the possibilities continue to grow. It is as though society has entered the world of *Star Trek*, when you consider that at least two companies offer a combination PDA and cell phone they call a *communicator*.[11] These hybrid devices come with a color screen, all the functions of both cell phones and PDAs, wireless Internet wherever service is available, on-demand e-mail, and Web surfing. Optional software makes it possible to work on Microsoft Word and Excel files that can be transferred to your computer. A frequent traveler program, photo album, chat function, and instant messaging make the communicator a fully loaded device for those who aspire to be "totally connected." Although these functions are neither ready for prime time nor universally available at affordable prices, most of us will have the opportunity to own one within a few years.

The PDA has earned a place on my list of top five "must have" digital tools for both personal and professional use. The list includes Internet and e-mail access, cell phone, PDA, digital camera, and portable computer. The digital camera will eventually work its way into the inventory of most people who work in the church simply because of the ability to capture images for use on websites, in presentations and electronic publications, as well as personal use. The laptop computer is especially valuable for those who travel and a necessity for bringing presentations to locations other than church or office. As computers continue to drop in price, the laptop computer as a second computer has become as normal as the family's second car did during the 1960s and 1970s. (But then again, who would have believed three-car garages would become standard in the suburbs!)

In addition to the five specific tools listed above, some of the most powerful professional resources are study and research sites available on the Internet. For sermon study and research, there are two valuable sites that have been around for several years. Five years' presence on the Internet is a long time; it is something like "dog years." Five years with a Web ministry connotes stability and excellence of product. Jenee Woodard's Textweek and Richard Fairchild's Sermons and Sermon-Lectionary Resources have extensive resources for preaching, and both have been active for just over five years.[12] My own Internet publication, Sermonhelp.com, actively published weekly sermons, exegetical notes, and worship helps for over five years.[13] Fairchild's Christmas and Easter pages are filled with an amazing amount of material that will enhance preparation for Advent and Christmas or Lenten and Easter programs, as well as extensive seasonal preaching helps. For study and reflection, the Christian Classics Ethereal Library has an absolutely stunning amount of material on classical Christian literature. As the website says, "There is enough good reading material here to last you a lifetime, if you give each work the time it deserves!"[14]

It will take some time to explore all that is available. Much of the religious material in cyberspace is just plain junk, but with time and patience you will discover a core of Internet sites that will become valuable resources for professional growth.

The last area of resources for professional development I want to mention is Bible software. Bible study software makes it possible to have Bibles and a virtual theological library available on your desktop computer. Every Christian leader will want to have at least one of these. There are several available, and I hesitate to declare one or another to be the most valuable, but I would offer the following tips. First of all, visit the Theophilos Bible Software website. Theophilos offers a free program that includes the King James Bible in full text as well as a number of free downloads to enhance the basic program. There are a number of very reasonably priced components available on CD, such as additional Bible versions, commentaries, devotional writings, and Bible dictionaries.[15] Other products worth checking out are available from Logos Bible Software, Parson's Technology, and Zondervan's Bible Study Library. Simply do a search on Google (www.google.com) for any of these companies or use the search terms, *Bible software*. The results will provide a day's worth of exploration. Be sure to look over each product carefully and take advantage of any free trials or downloads before you purchase. Any of these products will come with a learning curve, and chances are you will live with your choice for some time. With increasing competition and falling

prices, you will be able to invest in more than one program and mul-
tiply the resources available.

The Limits of Being Connected

Although interaction with technology is necessary, there are a few
words I would like to share with you on a more personal level as one
Christian leader to another (meaning all persons who are involved in
church work). We need to face the limits of how connected we can be in
a technological way and still maintain balance in a spiritual-theological
sense. If you should become the proud owner of a "communicator" and
qualify for the title "Totally Connected Christian Leader," you will want
to take time to reflect on these limits. Technology can make us more
available to persons in a number of ways. Yet, our availability to God,
family, and our own personal spiritual disciplines needs to come out
very high on our priority scale.

There are two subtle dangers that plague committed Christian
leaders who want to stay connected with community and current with
technology. First of all, we may find ourselves trapped in the need to
be so available to the community that we become unavailable to God
and family. Additionally, we find ourselves spending so much time with
technological accoutrements in order to serve the community that we
actually take time away from community. Everybody loses. God and
family are both disregarded as our availability is sucked into a black
hole. Time for personal spiritual discipline is nonexistent. This is no
academic issue. I found myself perilously close to this circumstance not
so long ago and came to a point of decision—the spiritual principles that
nourish my relationship with God, family, self, and community needed
to be set clearly at the top of my list of priorities. Rules for the use of
technological tools followed quickly. Each of us will need to fashion our
own approach, but these few principles were lifesavers for me:

- Limit the e-mail: My e-mail volume had grown to a point that a
  two- or three-day trip away from my computer was producing three
  hundred or more e-mail messages. Thus, I began to use an auto
  response saying, "I am out of the office until next Friday. If your
  e-mail is important, you should resend it after Friday. Due to the

volume of e-mail I receive, e-mail is automatically deleted while I am traveling." Perhaps there is some version of this you could use. I also let people know that I usually respond to e-mail within 48 hours. The principle here is to promise a certain response time and beat it. I actually answer e-mail within 24 hours when I am in town. Some people are very clear that they check e-mail two, three, or four times a week and that people should not expect a response beyond these limits. Also, tell people that if their question or inquiry would take more than five minutes in a telephone conversation, they should use the telephone instead of e-mail. One last rule is to make diligent use of common sense. If you get an e-mail from someone saying they are thinking of taking their life, forget the computer, get in your car, and go make a visit! Sometimes e-mail is not an appropriate way to be connected.

- Limit cell phone use: I make it clear that I do not carry a cell phone unless I am traveling. Even then, the cell phone is turned off at 9:00 P.M. and on again at 9:00 A.M. If I were serving a church as a pastor or in another leadership capacity, I would let the congregation know the hours that my cell phone was turned on. It is also important to be very public about personal spiritual and family commitments. My prayer time and family time now go into my PDA as appointments. My cell phone number is not available to others when I am on vacation. That is my time to be connected to God and family and nothing else.

- Practice technology fasting: I practice technology fasting one day a week. This means I deny myself access to all forms of technology including cell phones, computers, e-mail, and television. It would be great to say that this was an easy thing to do, but that would be untrue. I am a technology professional. I am waiting for the perfect "communicator" to arrive. My first few fast days with tech fasting were filled with hunger pangs. I was hungry to see who might have sent an e-mail and wanted to log on to see who had posted to my Pastoral Care class. But eventually, I became accustomed to the discipline of the "tech fast." God saw all that had been done in creation and said that it was good. Then God rested from all that was done. Similarly, all the technology enhancements to ministry are good. And it is also good to rest from all the technology and reconnect with the One who is the source of all genuine connection. If God considered rest, or Sabbath, to be important, why do we believe we are okay without it?

- Finally, in my own journey to become an authentically connected Christian leader who lives with technology every working day, I adopted a practice that helps to keep me balanced. Every morning when I arrive at work, I begin my day with a mini tech fast. I do not turn on my computer, do not check the messages the blinking red light on my phone set says are waiting, and do not check the appointment calendar on my PDA. Rather, I grab my worn, leather-bound Bible, a pad of lined paper, and wrap my fingers around a No. 2 pencil. While enjoying a few sips of Columbian Supreme coffee, I read the daily lectionary and make a few notes as to how the text speaks to my life at the moment.

- It was after two years of reading the daily lectionary online and working through my devotions on a PDA in the name of time management that I found myself closer to being more stressed out by technology than helped by it. It is then that I rediscovered the joy of pencil and paper, turning the pages of a physical Bible, and leaning back to reflect instead of leaning forward toward a computer screen. Once I have committed my notes to paper with the wonderful feel of a freshly sharpened No. 2 pencil, then it is "Katie, bar the door!" The computer screen comes to life, my PDA is placed in its interface cradle, and the e-mail begins its insistent nag; "Receiving, 1, 2, 3, 4 . . ."

Becoming a genuinely connected Christian leader has two learning curves. The first comes when you decide that you must become computer literate and begin to make use of all the digital resources that are a growing part of everyone's life. The second learning curve for those who enthusiastically embrace the digital revolution is this: The time will come when basic spiritual disciplines need to be rediscovered and placed at the center of ministry in a world that is seriously disconnected from God.

In the final chapter of this book, I will turn to the principles that will keep the focus of technology on the missional task of reaching a broken world. Technology as a "Golden Calf" does not serve the kingdom of

God well, but technology as servant of Christ can enable a bold foray into a pagan world on behalf of the kingdom. As we come to the end of this long conversation about ministry in a disconnected world, I want to explore in more detail those principles that will help pull the threads of our discussion together.

13

Putting It All Together— Principles for Successful Integration of Ministry and Technology

"The call here is for a church that will 'imitate' Christ to pitch tent, to embody itself, to take form in the indigenous practices of our time, not for the purpose of accommodation to the world but rather to be God's people."

Tex Sample[1]

We have taken a long journey through a not so simple territory filled with potential and riddled with mine-fields. Technology, science, ministry, and theology come together in new and exciting ways that energize and challenge us. There is so much to learn and so many ways to apply that learning. How do we put this all together in a way that is technologically responsible while maintaining theological integrity and actually making gains in ministry?

When the time comes to develop a comprehensive plan for integrating technology in your ministry context, there is a common old saying that contains important insight: The right hand doesn't know what the left hand is doing. This notion lies behind many of the pitfalls we have discussed throughout the book. As you move ahead, it will be essential to gain skill with digital technologies while at the same time applying important ministry principles, lest the technology overwhelm the ministry. Keeping the right and left hands working together means undertaking the *process* of engaging technology successfully while applying the three *principles* of vital ministry we discussed in chapter two. I want to explore briefly these twin peaks of ministry and technology, namely engaging technology and applying principles. In so doing, we will revisit some issues that have been discussed in previous chapters. Finally, I will offer a few last words of encouragement.

The Process of Engaging Technology

There are three stages that most people who are new to technology experience when they begin. The first experience is a scary sense of being overwhelmed. This has been true for many of our online students and faculty, as well as many who have attended Dubuque Seminary's technology conferences. The sense of being overwhelmed was especially evident in the Certificate in Ministry and Technology students at UDTS where the program begins with an intensive residency. The residency is a kind of baptism by fire. A second experience is that technology is no longer so overwhelming as it is mystifying. Working with new digital tools is like dwelling in an enchanted forest. What a *wonder*-full world this is! The third stage in the process of engaging technology comes when people become engrossed by it. The mystery fades a bit, and those who have persevered in learning the basics are energized by the incredible possibilities.

This is a dangerous point we have encountered a few times throughout this book. You *kind of* know what you are doing. Technology is no longer so overwhelming or mystifying, but you need to be aware that it does have invasive potential to take over your life. There was an example of this when the student in chapter ten said, "The Amish lifestyle sounds pretty good right now." It is at this point that the process of engaging technology will need the guiding hand of ministry principles. Without this balancing of the ministry-technology equation, the result will indeed be that the right hand doesn't know what the left hand is doing. In other words, the door is opened to the chaos discussed in chapter one.

The Process of Engaging Technology

Technology Is Overwhelming: When people first begin to work with technology in a ministry context, it is rather like deciding to take a vacation, pulling out a map of the entire United States, and asking, "Where should we go?" Most Americans have never visited a fraction of the nation. It would be overwhelming to ask, "Where should we go?" Several years ago, friends from England wrote to say they would be taking a two week "holiday" to the United States and said they would like to stop by. The visit would be short, however, because they really wanted to visit the Florida Everglades, Niagara Falls, the Redwood Forests, Mount Rushmore, the Grand Canyon, Lake Tahoe, New Orleans, Chicago, and New York City. *And* they planned to rent a van in order to best take in the sights. I explained something of the geography of the United States and told them about a six week trip I had taken to the West Coast from Chicago. There was hardly enough time to make the stops we wanted to in six weeks. My friends began to limit and fine tune their vacation plans. They found the possibilities overwhelming.

Technology is something like that. The pure scope of digital technologies is massive and becoming more so daily. There is simply too much to learn and too many areas where expertise is needed. There has been more than one occasion when I have been asked what kind of computer would be best for bringing film clips to worship. The question brings nothing but more questions. "How large is your sanctuary? Do you have an LCD projector, and if so, what is the 'throw' of the lens and how many lumens does the projector have? What kind of software do you plan to use for presentations?" And finally, "How many people will be working on your project?" And these questions are limited to using media in worship. There is so much to learn. The question that comes up most frequently with people who begin with interest in technology and then are overwhelmed by it all is, "How can I ever learn all this stuff?"

At this point it will be good to review the cautions about the regressive potential of technology in chapter one. Then we will revisit the brief planning primer in chapter five. Planning will bring order to the chaos of the seemingly untamed and overwhelming world of technology. There is an analogy with the world of sports when during a game you hear a commentator say about a fading team, "They need to get back to their game plan." If you do not have a game plan for technology in ministry, get one. If you do have a plan, stick to it, evaluate it, revise it, and *then* stick to it.

Technology Is Mystifying: A second kind of experience with technology happens when basic knowledge has been gained, and the world of digital technology becomes mystifying. When people get past the experience of being overwhelmed, they begin to understand just how much can be accomplished with new technologies. Technology actually has the potential to change an entire ministry in this brave new world of digital wonders. The key question people ask at this stage comes when they see what amazing things others are doing: "How do they do that?" This is truly a wonderful world. From amazing websites to incredible communication tools to transformed worship, we are in awe of what can be done. We are in the grip of the "wow" factor.

Almost daily, technology headlines tell new stories of technological advances that hold world-changing potential.[2] If Carnegie Mellon University professor Hans Moravec's work with a robotic vision system[3] reaches its potential, the 1987 film *RoboCop* will move from science fiction to reality. Moravec's book *Robot: Mere Machine to Transcendent Mind* suggests that intelligent robots will attain human levels of intelligence by 2040.[4] Whether or not this ever happens, the future shape of digital possibilities and the impact they will have is beyond imagining.

When we begin to work on ways to apply the wonders of technology to our ministry context, we begin to move from being mystified to becoming fully engaged.

Technology Is Engrossing: After being overwhelmed—"How can I learn all this stuff?"—and moving through the mystery—"How do *they* do that?"—the third stage in the process of engaging technology is reached when we begin to work toward specific application of technologies in ministry. Now the primary question is, "How do *I* do that?"

This is at once the most promising and the most precarious point of the journey. It is promising because of the potential that exists and the good gains that can be made for ministry. This is also a precarious time because engagement with technology and all its demands and learning curves can throw our lives out of balance. The specific application of technology to new ministry situations is a challenging experience. This is the point at which the sense of urgency and chronic alarm discussed in chapter four can take root.

The process of engaging technology will have the optimum chance of being a positive experience when the following ministry principles are allowed to be the senior partners of the ministry and technology enterprise.

The Principles of Vital Ministry

I want to now revisit the principles of ministry first discussed in chapter two. You will recall that *particularity* addresses the issue of who we are as God's people, and *intentionality* moves the people of God into the world. That is to say, *who* we are in Christ shapes *how* we are in the world. Finally, *mutuality* is the glue that holds everything together in the body of Christ.

Particularity: One of the key mistakes made by congregations and their leaders is trying to "do church" the way others do it. Every church and ministry has its own unique personality. As with human beings who are uniquely created by God, so also the church is a unique, specific body of persons unlike any other body. Just as there ought not to be "cookie cutter" Christians, so there should be no assembly line churches. When churches seek to imitate the ministry of other groups, the result will almost always be counterproductive. One pastor I spoke with who had attended workshops and conferences on church revitalization said, "I have attended several conferences on church renewal and have returned home more discouraged each time." He had visited churches that were experiencing vitality and growth and were in turn holding conferences to show other churches how to do it. The problem is that unlike the Michael Jordan "be like Mike" commercials you may have seen on television, when we attempt to be like other persons or other congregations, the result is almost always discouraging. Franchises are best left to the fast food chains and department stores.

The New Testament letters make it abundantly clear that each church is unique. Each has unique problems and unique opportunities. Amazingly, Paul found something positive to say to almost every congregation he wrote to. And that was no easy thing to do. Corinth was filled with divisions, and the Galatian churches were ready to trade in the gospel of grace and freedom for the old religion of law and bondage. Yet Corinth had a strong commitment to knowing Christ and using spiritual gifts and expectantly waited for the coming of Christ.[5] One can imagine a number of ways contemporary technologies might serve the ministry of the Corinthian church. The churches of Galatia, however, are another story. After an initial greeting, Paul moves immediately into shock and dismay over the way they have been moved from the vital center of faith, namely the grace of God in Jesus Christ. It is difficult to think of any way technologies could do anything in that situation until the churches of Galatia were able to recenter themselves in the basics of Christian faith. The principle of particularity would help them focus on who they were and perhaps help them rediscover their roots. Technology might aid in the process, but nothing could happen that could advance the kingdom of God until they knew who they were as God's people. We saw this in chapter one where technology opened up opportunities for all kinds of spiritual distortion.

There are no shortcuts. The successful application of technology in ministry requires the same commitment of time and energy as any other ministry in the church. The questions of identity that are posed by the principle of particularity will blend well with the initial planning discussed in chapter five. The planning and work done in light of the unique identity of a congregation is the equivalent of building one's house on a rock instead of on sand (Matt. 7:24–27). Planning and particularity go together. My prediction is that a large percentage of churches that become involved with technology, whether it be through a website, media in worship, or in other venues, will eventually walk away from the program. Many will say the technology did not work, but the fact will be that they did not properly work the technology.

Intentionality: Intentionality moves the discussion of *who* we are as the people of God into *how* we go about expressing this identity in the world around us. If we conceptualize our particular group as *God's*

Journeying People, we will likely use the theme of spiritual journey in our outreach and in the expression of worship. If there is a website, the journey theme will be evident. Another group might see itself in terms of a *Faithful Remnant*, and the expressions of the life of the church might well lift up the ideals of committed living and serious discipleship. Being intentional about identity will give shape to how Web ministry, media in worship, or outreach through online community is accomplished. In chapter five, one of the essential points for initial technology planning was to involve all of the stakeholders in planning for the church's technology ministry. The stakeholders are, of course, all the people in the church. Being intentional means bringing all of the stakeholders on board with the church's expression of its mission. This ties in with the concept of missional direction discussed in chapter twelve and the possibilities for evangelism using digital technologies. When the ministry and technology program of the church or ministry group is intentional, it is theologically thinking through how it will "be God's people" in Jerusalem, Judea, Samaria, Chicago, San Antonio, and the ends of the earth. The section on "Thinking Theologically" in chapter two will help your group reflect on how it will use technology to express its identity in mission.

Mutuality: Mutuality provides a reality check for the first two principles and the concept that will hold the feet of all parties to the fire of theological-spiritual integrity in your integration of ministry and technology. Whether it be the church's website, development of a media ministry, or revisioning a confirmation program using technology, the principle of mutuality is at the heart of the efforts.

We are most authentically the church, the body of Christ, when all the parts of the body are involved in using gifts for ministry. Throughout this book, especially in the discussion of community in chapter two, the idea of every person having a part in ministry and gifts to build up the body of Christ is a central concept. I have suggested that the demands of using technology appropriately in ministry requires the assistance of many persons, and thus, may provide us with a way to contribute to the revitalization of lay ministry in the contemporary church. The multimedia worship service and team approach of Union-Congregational Church is an example of how mutuality in ministry is the very heartbeat of both ministry and technology as a field. It shows what the church has been called to be from the beginning.

If all of us who call ourselves by the name of Christ are not ministers, then none of us are ministers in a truly biblical sense of the word "minister."

Last Words

In chapter five, I made the brief suggestion that maybe it would be best that you forget about technology. While that suggestion was somewhat tongue in cheek, the fact is that none of us can escape the digital revolution. I do believe that we must have the strongest caution toward the notion of technology as messianic. If you have the idea that technology will somehow "save the day," then my hope is that you will focus on the three ministry principles discussed here and take time for serious discussion of them with your leadership before you move ahead.

Some of you may have come to this text with a fair amount of experience and expertise in the field of technology. My hope for you is that this book has in some sense taken you back to the drawing board in a way that you will realize technology without theology is a tragedy for the church. We do need you and your expertise in order to make use of the full potential of this field to reach our generation. And *you* need the corrective lens of theological-spiritual reflection to be sure that the potential is squarely aimed at making disciples who will become agents of God's kingdom.

My deepest desire is that many of you who are new to the prospect of using digital technologies in ministry will be reassured, and that any trepidation you are feeling will be alleviated. I trust that you will be encouraged in the sense of "taking courage" to move ahead in this work. Many of you who are called "newbies" by the tech people will actually become the vanguard of committed people from the mainstream church in America who will bring the use of digital technology to "the rest of us." Our ministry and technology programs at Dubuque Seminary have an informal motto. That motto is "Technology for Everybody." We believe that the greatest gains for God's kingdom using digital technologies have not yet been made. They will not be made by the "Headliners and Legends" of the contemporary Christian world. They will be made in the trenches of small, medium, and larger churches where people are seeking not so much the spectacular as the substantive.

I trust that you will join with me in being optimistic about the promise of technology even as you are concerned about its pitfalls. You will become a part of those who will successfully navigate the pitfalls and realize the potential—because the kingdom demands it. Be patient as you learn, persistent as you work, and prayerful as you succeed.

Notes

Introduction

1. *Little Oxford Dictionary of Quotations*, (http://www.askoxford.com/quotations/627). Accessed February 14, 2003.

2. Walter P. Wilson, *The Internet Church* (Nashville: Word, 2000), xii.

3. Ibid. See also, Andrew Carega, *eMinistry: Connecting with the Net Generation* (Grand Rapids: Kregel, 2001).

4. A prime example is Ginghamsburgh United Methodist Church in Tipp, Ohio, (http://www.ginghamsburg.org).

5. Wilson, *The Internet Church*, xi.

6. Carega, *eMinistry*,16.

7. Roosevelt's speech is available at the National Archives and Records Administration, (http://www.nara.gov/education/teaching/fdr/infamy.html). Accessed January 18, 2002. The website is a part of the National Archives and Records Administration's Digital Classroom initiative. It provides educators with outstanding opportunities for using electronic resources in the classroom at all educational levels. The Digital Classroom website is located at (http://www.nara.gov/education/classrm.html). Accessed January 18, 2002.

8. University of San Diego History of Radio website, *Golden Age of Radio 1935-50*, (http://history.acusd.edu/gen/recording/radio2.html). Revised March 7, 2001; accessed January 18, 2002. Main page for the History of Radio site is at (http://history.acusd.edu/gen/recording/radio.html).

9. National Archives and Records Administration, *NARA Online*, (http://www.nara.gov/education/teaching/fdr/infamy.html).

10. See the definition of nanosecond along with related links to nanotechnology at *Webopedia's* website: (http://www.xphomestation.com/news.html). Accessed January 20, 2002.

11. Tom Crews, *XP Pony Express Homepage*, (http://www.xphomestation.com/). Accessed January 20, 2002.

12. Ibid. (http://www.xphomestation.com/frm-history.html). Accessed February 7, 2002.

13. Hebrew *rachaph*, *NIV Bible Commentary*, Zondervan Reference Software, 1994.

Chapter 1

1. Susan J. White, *Christian Worship and Technological Change* (Nashville: Abingdon, 1994), 112.

2. Dave Gussow, "Bad Calls," *The St. Petersburg Times Online News*, 30 April 2001, (http://www.sptimes.com/News/043001/Technology/Bad_calls.shtml). Accessed February 24, 2002.

3. At least not yet! There is the possibility that the cell phone could be combined with a wireless PDA that would have the potential to download sermon notes and Scripture quotations even as the sermon was being delivered. PowerPoint presentations could also be downloaded, messages from the nursery to parents could be sent. Parents could set their cell phones to vibrate instead of ring and the nursery could reach them during worship. Trust me—someone will do all these things somewhere someday.

4. Wilson, *The Internet Church*, 15.

5. Carega, *eMinistry*, 22.

6. The *Scientology Home Page*, (http://www.scientology.org/home.html). Accessed March 1, 2002. See also the *Guide to Cults* website, (http://www.factnet.org/). Accessed March 1, 2002. This site has a large amount of information on Scientology.

7. Quentin J. Schultze, "What We've Learned So Far: A Sober Assessment of Web Evangelism in the Light of Seven Years Experience" (lecture presented at the annual meeting of the Internet Evangelism Coalition, Rosemont, Ill., 18 September 2002).

8. About.com, *Pagan/Wiccan Religion*, (http://paganwiccan.about.com/mbody.htm). Accessed March 3, 2002.

9. California Astrology Association, *Spellcasting by Andreika the Witch*, (http://www.spellmasters.com/spells.html). Accessed March 3, 2002.

10. Universal Life Church, *Universal Life Church Online*, (http://ulc.net/). Revised August 25, 2002; accessed March 3, 2002.

11. Ibid. (http://www.ulc.net/shop/).

12. Dennis A. Smith and B. F. Gutierrez, "In the Power of the Spirit," *Religion Online*. (http://www.religion-online.org/cgi-bin/relsearchd.dll/showbook?item_id=374). Accessed March 1, 2002.

13. (http://news.com.com/2100-1023-240741.html?legacy=cnet). Accessed February 10, 2003.

14. Matt Welch, "My Time in the DEN of Iniquity," *USC Annenburg Online Journalism Review*, 4 April 2002, (http://www.ojr.org/ojr/workplace/1017964454.php).

Chapter 2

1. Dietrich Bonhoeffer, *Life Together*, (New York: Harper and Brothers, 1954), 21.

2. Ibid., 31 note 1. We use the terminology of John W. Doberstein, translator of Bonhoeffer's book in translating *geistlich* as *spiritual* and *seelisch* as *human* rather than the more precise terms *pneumatic* and *psychic*.

3. Ibid., 31.

4. Len Wilson and Jason Moore, *Digital Storytellers: The Art of Communicating the Gospel in Worship* (Nashville: Abingdon, 2002), 16.

5. Terry Lindvall, *The Silents of God* (London: Scarecrow, 2001), 46.

6. Ibid., 47.

7. Andrew Odlyzko, "Content is Not King," *First Monday: Peer-Reviewed Journal on the Internet,* (http://www.firstmonday.dk/issues/issue6_2/odlyzko/). Accessed July 10, 2002. This is a good discussion of the "Content" issue and exploration of the future of the Internet. The article is a provocative critique of the long-term impact of the Internet.

Chapter 3

1. Quentin Schultze, *Habits of the High-Tech Heart: Living Virtuously in the Information Age* (Grand Rapids: Baker Academic, 2002), 191.

2. (http://www.augustachronicle.com/stories/060799/tec_124-2786.shtml). *The Augusta Chronicle Online*, Web posted June 7, 1999, accessed February 14, 2003.

3. AT&T Wireless. *Welcome to mlife*, (http://www.attws.com). Accessed September 13, 2002.

4. Donald Tapscott, *Growing Up Digital* (New York: McGraw Hill, 1999), 7.

5. *MMORPG Café*, 20 July 2002, (http://www.mmorpgcafe.com/). Accessed September 13, 2002.

6. Jon Frankel, "Everquest or Evercrack?" *CBS News Early Show*, 28 May 2002, (http://www.cbsnews.com/stories/2002/05/28/earlyshow/contributors/earlyshow/contributors/jonfrankel/main510302.shtml). Accessed September 13, 2002.

7. Ibid.

8. Ibid.

9. Ibid.

Chapter 4

1. John Mueller, "Technology and Stress," 8 November 2001, (http://mueller.educ.ucalgary.ca/TS2001/). Accessed September 7, 2002.

2. (http://peer.tamu.edu/curriculum_modules/OrganSystems/Coordination/storytime.htm). Accessed February 14, 2003.

3. The McGraw Hill Companies, *Biography: Hans Selye*, (http://www.dushkin.com/connectext/psy/ch12/bio12.mhtml). Accessed September 8, 2002.

4. Ann Barbour, "Got A Life," in the *Online Observer*, 29 January 2001, http://www.nd.edu/~observer/01292001/Viewpoint/1.html. Accessed August 26, 2003.

5. Schultze, *Habits of the High-Tech Heart*, 18.

6. From the *Christian Computing Magazine* website: (http://www.ccmag.com). At the webwite, choose the CCMag Store link on the left side navigation bar. The

direct link at the time of this writing is: (http://www.ccmag.com/templates/cusccmag/details.asp?id=22104&PID=57055). Accessed February 14, 2003.

7. See the article on Luddism at the University of Colorado, Denver School of Education website at: (http://carbon.cudenver.edu/~mryder/itc_data/luddite.html). Accessed February 10, 2003.

8. About.Com, Urban Legends and Folklore, "Bill Gates is the Antichrist!" Updated June 15, 1998, (http://urbanlegends.about.com/library/blgates2.htm). Accessed October 4, 2002. The argument is also debunked on this page. For more on this myth enter "Bill Gates 666" into a search engine. There will be hundreds of "hits."

9. "The 2003 Fortune 500," *Fortune*, (http//www.fortune.com/fortune/fortune500). Accessed April 21, 2003.

10. PowerPoint is either a registered trademark or trademark of Microsoft Corporation in the United States and/or other countries.

Chapter 5

1. Quoted from the I-Hate-Computers.org website article, "Why do I need a computer," (http://www.i-hate-computers.org/why.html). Accessed October 21, 2002.

2. John Jewell, *New Tools For a New Century: First Steps in Equipping your Church for the Digital Revolution* (Nashville: Abingdon, 2001). Chapters nine and twelve are especially germane to the issue of planning.

3. Netscape and the Netscape N and Ship's Wheel logos are registered trademarks of Netscape Communications Corporation in the United States and other countries, (http://www.netscape.com).

4. One good resource is Roy M. Oswald and Robert E. Friedrich, Jr., *Discerning Your Congregation's Future: A Strategic and Spiritual Approach* (Washington, D.C.: Alban Institute, 1996).

5. There is an extensive planning guide on the Apple website that is intended for use by educational institutions but can be well used by churches and other ministries. Visit (http://www.apple.com/education) for more information.

6. "Imaging at Penn State: One Solution, Multiple Variations," *Syllabus Magazine* (October 2002): 44.

7. Schultze's keynote address given September 17, 2002, at the annual meeting of the Internet Evangelism Coalition in Rosemont, Illinois.

8. Avoid using a hit counter on your website. They detract from the look and feel of the site and may simply tell people no one is visiting. You wouldn't put a sign in front of the church that said, "No one visited here last month." If you want to do a website analysis, try a Web stats service such as (http://www.goldstats.com). If you do use such a service, pay the extra price to get rid of banners.

9. Visit (www.sundaysoftware.com) for excellent hardware and software advice.

10. Our Ministry and Technology students at the University of Dubuque Theological Seminary have rated Webopedia as one of the most helpful websites they have used in their work and study.

Chapter 6

1. The American Institute of Physics, "Physics Creates Jobs," (http://www.aip.org/success/createsjobs/). Accessed October 12, 2002.

2. Ibid.

3. Twain quote by Dr. David E. Shi, President of Furman University, (http://www.furman.edu/president/column14.htm). Accessed February 14, 2003.

4. The American Institute of Physics, "From R&D to Widespread Utility," (http://www.aip.org/success/createsjobs/index.html). Accessed October 13, 2002.

5. Robert H'obbes' Zakon, Hobbes' Internet Timeline, (http://www.zakon.org/robert/internet/timeline/). Updated February 5, 2003.

6. CyberAtlas Staff, "Internet Population Continues to Grow," (http://cyberatlas.internet.com/big_picture/geographics/article/0,,5911_969541,00.html). Accessed October 13, 2002.

7. Walt Wilson, "The Internet Moment in History," (http://www.ccmag.com/templates/cusccmag/details.asp?id=22104&PID=64880&mast=). Accessed October 13, 2002.

8. There is a Web tour available that has been used with the Dubuque Theological Seminary Certificate in Ministry and Technology students. See (http://www.udtslearning.net/CMTwebtour.htm). Many websites come and go. This tour was still available at the time of publication.

9. ReligiousResources.org, *Religious Resources on the Internet*, (http://www.religiousresources.org/). Accessed October 14, 2002.

10. ReligiousResources.org, *Web Site Development for Religious Organizations*, (http://religiousresources.org/homepage/about.php). Accessed October 14, 2002.

11. Visit (www.buydomains.com) for complete information.

12. See Jewell, *New Tools For a New Century*, chapter one, for basic information on how the Internet works.

13. Blogger.com, Push-Button Publishing for the People, (http://www.Blogger.com).

14. Visit (http://www.ezboard.com) for more information on this product.

15. Visit (http://www.infopop.com) for more information. As of this writing, the cost of the most popular bulletin board software, UBB Classic, was $199.

16. The chat room used by First Church is provided by (www.raidersoft.com). Visit to explore the services that are available.

17. From the website of the Internet Evangelism Coalition, (http://www.gospelcom.net/bgc/iec/about.html). Accessed October 17, 2002.

18. Try the websites at: (http://www.nowtrygod.com), (http://www.adhim.com), and (http://www.growinginchrist.com).

19. Here are two recommendations for graphics software: Adesign, (http://pierresoft.com/eng/) and PhotoImpact (http://www.ulead.com/).

Chapter 7

1. James B. Finley, Autobiography (1853), 178. Quoted in Frederick Norwood, *The Story of American Methodism* (Nashville: Abingdon, 1974), 131.

2. The Journal of John Wesley, published on the excellent Christian Classics Ethereal website, (http://www.ccel.org/w/wesley/journal/htm/vi.htm). Accessed October 23, 2002.

3. Norwood, *Story of American Methodism,* 130.

4. The password function is a JavaScript that can easily be placed on a page. There are many scripts like this available free at: (http://www.javascript.com/).

5. Information for this product is located at: (http://www.infopop.com/products/ubbclassic/).

6. Information for this product is located at: (http://freechat.raidersoft.com/).

7. MSN is available at: (http://messenger.msn.com/). AOL is available at: (http://www.aim.com/).

Chapter 8

1. C. S. Lewis, *Surprised by Joy* (New York: Harcourt, Brace Jovanovich, 1955), 181.

2. (www.kfki.hu/~arthp/art/b/barocci/egypt.jpg).

3. (http://www.kfki.hu/~arthp/html/e/elsheime/egypt-e.html).

4. (www.mfa.org/artemis/fullrecord.asp?oid=31734&did=500).

5. *How the Grinch Stole Christmas,* 1966, Warner Home Video.

6. In "Light Shows of the Mind," David Brooks states: "A crucial point here is that the imagination is amphibious. It lives in the worlds of both reason and fantasy. It always seems to be pushing us toward some product or benefit. . . . For example, our imaginations trick us into undertaking difficult tasks. We decide to learn a language, renovate our house, move to a new town, have children, or begin writing a book. We envision the pleasure and satisfaction we will feel and the success we will achieve. Then those tasks turn out to be hard, and the difficulties we encounter bring out our best exertions and make us better people." *Atlantic Monthly* (December 2002): 30–31. Although it is not the task that Brooks envisions, what project is more difficult than losing one's life so that one might find true life?

7. Peter Matheson, *The Imaginative World of the Reformation* (Minneapolis: Fortress, 2001), 6.

8. See Karl Barth's "The Strange New World Within the Bible," in *The Word of God and the Word of Man* (Gloucester: Peter Smith, 1978), 28–50. Although Barth does not cite the imagination itself in this famous essay, he certainly illustrates the Scripture's power to destroy old worlds and create new ones.

9. Andrew Greeley, *The Catholic Imagination* (Berkeley: University of California Press, 2000), 9.

10. Ibid.

11. Lewis, *Surprised by Joy,* 181.

12. And I'm quite sure invokes many other messages as well!

Chapter 9

1. Nancy Lammers Gross, *If You Can't Preach Like Paul* (Grand Rapids: Eerdmans, 2002), 37.

2. The Certificate in Ministry and Technology website is: (http://www.udtslearning.net/CMT/CMT.htm).

3. One example is Fowler Productions. Their website includes information on multimedia workshops: (http://www.fowlerinc.com/).

4. Rev. Wade Kirsteatter, CMT Project Proposal, August 2002.

5. Rev. William Taylor, CMT Project Proposal, August 2002.

6. Rev. Dr. James C. Dunkin, Senior Pastor, First Presbyterian Church, Lawrence, Kansas.

7. Melvin J. Steinbron, *Can the Pastor Do It Alone?* (Ventura, Ca.: Regal, 1987).

8. Rev. James Wakelin, Bloomfield Christian Church, Bloomfield, Iowa. In an e-mail sent Wednesday, November 6, 2002, 7:00 A.M.

9. William Taylor, in an e-mail message, sent November 13, 2002.

Chapter 10

1. Sally Morgenthaler, *Worship Evangelism: Inviting Unbelievers into the Presence of God* (Grand Rapids: Zondervan, 1995), 18.

2. I have chosen not to name these churches, but there are many you can check out in the nearest large city.

3. Michael Bausch, *Silver Screen, Sacred Story* (Bethesda, Md.: Alban Institute, 2002), 18. Dr. Bausch teaches in the Certificate in Ministry and Technology program of Dubuque Seminary. His area of specialty is multimedia worship.

4. Larry Withham, *The State of Grace: Small Churches Face Challenges*, (http://www.uscongregations.org/washtime.htm). Accessed, November 25, 2002.

5. See the U.S. Congregational Life Survey online at: (http://www.uscongregations.org/). The site has valuable information and offers a report entitled *A Field Guide to U.S. Congregations* published by Westminster John Knox Press.

6. Information on the pasty as well as online ordering is available at: (http://www.dobberspasties.com/index.php). Accessed, November 26, 2002.

7. *Escanaba in Da Moonlight*, 2000, Monarch Home Video.

8. From the Eagle's album, *Hell Freezes Over*, a collection of Eagle's hits from the 1970s as well as four new songs (Geffen, 1994).

9. See Bausch's book, *Silver Screen, Sacred Story*, for details on budget-friendly equipment and set up.

10. I want to express heartfelt thanks to Rich and Teri Dary who are core members of the team that has led the church in its multimedia worship. Teri has joined our adjunct faculty at Dubuque Seminary teaching in the Certificate in Ministry and Technology program.

11. Richard Dary in a conversation after the Thanksgiving service, November 24, 2002.

Chapter 11

1. Quoted in Lindvall, *The Silents of God*, 153.

2. See ch. 6 note 6. CyberAtlas is the finest resource for Internet demographics I have found.

3. Ibid.

4. Ibid., 151.

5. Ibid., 153.

6. Ibid., 161. Lindvall's book is an important contribution to the study of Technology and Ministry. Many of the themes parallel the current dialogue in the use of technology in the life of the church.

7. The church's website details the story of the church. The address is: (www.bridgetogod.org).

8. Ruth Tucker, *Walking Away From Faith* (Downer's Grove, Ill.: InterVarsity Press, 2002).

9. Visit the site at: (www.questioningfaith.com).

10. The Web address is: (http://cweb.gospelcom.net/).

11. (http://www.gospelcom.net/guide/).

12. Visit Youth Specialties at: (http://www.youthspecialties.com/).

13. Visit (www.pinnaclesys.com) for software for the PC and (www.apple.com) for the Macintosh version. The Macintosh comes with iMovie 2, which is a very good editing system.

Chapter 12

1. Robert L. Conly, "New Miracles of the Telephone Age," *National Geographic Magazine* (July 1954): 87. (Harold Osborne, chief engineer for AT&T, made this prediction in 1954.)

2. This took place in 1948 in Northern Ontario where the road turned west to Kenora, Ontario. Hearing how technology came to our area, my oldest son once asked if I knew Abraham Lincoln. It wasn't that I lived in the "olden days" so much as it was that technology came to us about twenty-five to fifty years behind the rest of the world. The rest of the world began about 700 miles to the south in Toronto, Ontario.

3. Vincent Ryan and Susan Kalla, *Telephony Online Magazine*, (http://currentissue.telephonyonline.com/ar/telecom_susan_kalla/). Accessed November 30, 2002. Susan Kalla joined FBR & Co., Inc. in May 2001 as a senior vice president and senior analyst covering the telecommunications industry.

4. For a basic computer literacy primer visit the website: (http://aalrc.org/cl/welcome.html). Accessed December 6, 2002. The site is sponsored by the Arkansas Adult Learning Resource Center. See also chapters one and two in Jewell, *New Tools For a New Century*.

5. See ch. 6 note 6. CyberAtlas Staff, *U.S. Internet Population Continues To Grow.* Accessed December 6, 2002.

6. *The Daily Office:* (http://www.missionstclare.com/english/index.html). Accessed December 6, 2002.

7. Universalis: (http://www.universalis.com/cgi-bin/display/). Accessed December 6, 2002.

8. Gospelcom, "Our Daily Bread: Attempting the Impossible," (http://www.gospelcom.net/rbc/odb/odb.shtml). Accessed December 7, 2002.

9. See an example of available resources at the Gospelcom site: (http://www.gospelcom.net/services/pda/). Accessed December 7, 2002.

10. For more information on the PDA, visit the PDA tutorial at: (http://www.youthspecialties.com/articles/puter/2001/february/column.php). Accessed December 7, 2002.

11. As of this writing, Handspring and Nokia offer the "communicator."

12. Textweek is located at: (www.textweek.com). Sermons and Sermon-Lectionary Resources is at: (http://www.rockies.net/~spirit/sermon.html).

13. The site was published for just over five years and CDs are still available with lectionary-based material covering years A, B, and C. Visit (www.Sermonhelp.com).

14. Christian Classics Ethereal Library: (http://www.ccel.org/).

15. Visit Theophilos at: (http://www.theophilos.sk/).

Chapter 13

1. Tex Sample, *The Spectacle of Worship in a Wired World* (Nashville: Abingdon, 1998), 122.

2. See the technology headline page of the CMT program of Dubuque Seminary at: (http://www.udtslearning.net/CMT/CMTTechHeadlines.htm).

3. From an article on the website of CNet News.com by Ed Frauenheim, titled "Giving Robots the Gift of Sight," (http://news.com.com/2100-1040-978854.html?tag=fd_top). Accessed December 31, 2002.

4. Hans Moravec, *Robot: Mere Machine to Transcendent Mind* (London: Oxford University Press, 2000). From the back cover.

5. 1 Corinthians 1:4–7.